PERFECT OUTDOOR GAS GRIDDLE

A Barbecuing & Grilling Cookbook

By Matt Jason

healthy happy Foodie

HHF Press

San Francisco

REVIEWS

> By the looks of the instructions it looks simple and easy to use. I liked the illustrated instructions and quick start chapter!
>
> **Sabrina S.**

> After some grill basics, such as how to use the various buttons and controls, I was surprised to find some "pro tips" I hadn't thought of, and a ton of recipes that look appetizing and fun. Nice collection!
>
> **Camilla V.**

> For an outdoor grill junkie like me, I found this book to have some fantastic recipes! I also really appreciated the 10 Minute fast start chapter — it should be in the actual manual from the manufacturer.
>
> **Gilly A.**

> This book came as a gift with my new grill. I quickly realized it's not from the manufacturer, but I like it better because it seems more straightforward and, dare I say, more useful than the guide that came with the grill. The recipes cover a lot of territory...I'm pleasantly surprised.
>
> **Dave B.**

> Wow, this book came in handy! I had to prepare for a big BBQ party and I found some excellent ideas that made the party a huge success. Consider the recipes for sandwiches and desserts, they're pretty amazing actually. Who would have thought of making a peach and berry pizza on a grill? It's amazing!
>
> **Armand S.**

INTRODUCTION

WHO THIS BOOK IS FOR?

If you have just purchased, or already own, a gas grill, then you need this book! Here's why:

GET THE MOST OUT OF YOUR GAS GRILL!

Illustrated instructions, a quick start guide and beyond-the-manual tips and tricks will teach you how to get the most out of your grill so that it becomes your family's favorite way to cook outdoors.

GET A FAST START WITH "10 MINUTE QUICK-START!"

Our illustrated "10 Minute Quick-Start" chapter will walk you through your first complete meals in under 10 minutes, so you can quickly enjoy delicious burgers, steaks, vegetables, and more instead of spending all of your time reading instruction manuals.

CLEAR, ILLUSTRATED INSTRUCTIONS.

We'll make using a gas grill so simple you can start cooking in minutes while avoiding beginner mistakes such as wrong heat, wrong ingredients, food sticking to the grill, etc.

GO BEYOND THE INSTRUCTION MANUAL.

Our Pro tips will have you cooking like the pro's in no time. Learn the science behind perfectly grilled food so that you can confidently make the best, most nutritious outdoor meals you've ever had.

UNBIASED RECOMMENDATIONS, WORKAROUNDS, AND PRO TIPS.

To help you confidently make amazing meals that are perfectly tailored to your family, while avoiding common mistakes, wherever you go!

ALL THE RECIPES YOU'LL EVER NEED!

101 of the best recipes on the planet will allow you to make the classic BBQs, lunches, and dinners you are already familiar with, as well as fun and exciting recipes which will give your family the variety they love.

CONTENTS

- 1 ABOUT THE FLAT TOP GRIDDLE
- 7 HOW TO USE A GAS GRIDDLE
- 12 10 MINUTE QUICK-START
- 15 PRO TIPS
- 21 **BREAKFAST**
  - 22 Classic French Toast
  - 23 Classic Buttermilk Pancakes
  - 24 Fluffy Blueberry Pancakes
  - 26 Simple French Crepes
  - 27 Classic Denver Omelette
  - 28 Bacon and Gruyere Omelette
  - 29 Bacon Egg and Cheese Sandwich
  - 30 Sausage and Vegetable Scramble
  - 31 Classic Steak and Eggs
  - 32 Toad in a Hole
  - 33 Ultimate Breakfast Burrito
  - 34 Mexican Scramble
  - 35 Hash Brown Scramble
  - 36 Golden Hash Browns
  - 37 Potato Bacon Hash
- 39 **SANDWICHES & BREADS**
  - 40 Tangy Chicken Sandwiches
  - 41 Savory Chicken Burgers
  - 42 Sun-Dried Tomato and Chicken Flatbreads
  - 43 Turkey Pesto Panini
  - 45 Classic American Burger
  - 46 Layered Beef & Corn Burger
  - 47 Cheesy Ham and Pineapple Sandwich
  - 48 Croque Madame
  - 49 Salmon Burgers
  - 50 Ultimate Grilled Cheese
  - 52 Garlic Parmesan Grilled Cheese Sandwiches
  - 53 Grilled Pizza Cheese
  - 54 Mini Portobello Burgers
  - 55 Veggie Pesto Flatbread
  - 56 Grilled Vegetable Pizza
  - 57 Bacon Jalapeno Wraps
- 59 **MAIN DISHES: POULTRY**
  - 61 Classic BBQ Chicken
  - 62 California Seared Chicken
  - 63 Sweet Chili Lime Chicken
  - 64 Seared Spicy Citrus Chicken
  - 65 Honey Balsamic Marinated Chicken
  - 66 Salsa Verde Marinated Chicken
  - 67 Hasselback Stuffed Chicken
  - 68 Creole Chicken Stuffed With Cheese & Peppers
  - 69 Root Beer Can Chicken
  - 70 Chipotle Adobe Chicken
  - 71 Sizzling Chicken Fajitas
  - 73 Chicken Tacos With Avocado Crema
  - 74 Hawaiian Chicken Skewers
  - 75 Fiery Italian Chicken Skewers
  - 76 Chicken Thighs With Ginger-Sesame Glaze
  - 77 Honey Sriracha Grilled Chicken Thighs

78 Chicken Wings with Sweet Red Chili and Peach Glaze
79 Yellow Curry Chicken Wings
80 Korean Grilled Chicken Wings With Scallion
81 Kale Caesar Salad With Seared Chicken
82 Buffalo Chicken Wings
84 Seared Chicken With Fruit Salsa
85 Teriyaki Chicken And Veggie Rice Bowls
86 Chicken Satay with Almond Butter Sauce
87 Chicken Fried Rice

89 MAIN DISHES: BEEF

91 Basic Juicy NY Strip Steak
92 High-Low Strip Steak
93 Tuscan-Style Steak with Crispy Potatoes
94 Caprese Grilled Filet Mignon
95 Rib-Eye Steak with Herbed Steak Butter
96 Teppanyaki Beef with Vegetables
98 Tender Steak with Pineapple Rice
99 Caprese Flank Steak
100 Flank Steak with Garlic and Rosemary
101 Greek Flank Steak Gyros
103 Texas-Style Brisket
104 Flash-Marinated Skirt Steak
105 Coffee Crusted Skirt Steak
106 Carne Asada
107 Mexican Steak Salad

109 MAIN DISHES: PORK

110 Pork Tenderloin Sandwiches
112 Herb-Crusted Mediterranean Pork Tenderloin
113 Paprika Dijon Pork Tenderloin
114 Moroccan Spiced Pork Tenderloin with Creamy Harissa Sauce
115 Sticky-Sweet Pork Shoulder
117 Grilled Pork Chops with Herb Apple Compote
118 Yucatan-Style Grilled Pork
119 Pineapple Bacon Pork Chops
120 Glazed Country Ribs
122 Garlic Soy Pork Chops
123 Honey Soy Pork Chops
125 Habanero-Marinated Pork Chops
126 Cuban Pork Chops
127 Spicy Cajun Pork Chops

129 MAIN DISHES: SEAFOOD

130 Salmon Fillets with Basil Butter & Broccolini
131 Spiced Snapper with Mango and Red Onion Salad
132 Honey-Lime Tilapia and Corn Foil Pack
133 Halibut Fillets with Spinach and Olives
134 Spiced Crab Legs
136 Gremolata Swordfish Skewers
137 Lobster Tails with Lime Basil Butter
138 Lump Crab Cakes
139 Spicy Grilled Jumbo Shrimp
141 Coconut Pineapple Shrimp Skewers
142 Mexican Shrimp Tacos
143 Bacon Wrapped Scallops
144 Scallops with Lemony Salsa Verde
145 Grilled Oysters with Spiced Tequila Butter
146 Pop-Open Clams with Horseradish-Tabasco Sauce
147 Spicy Grilled Squid

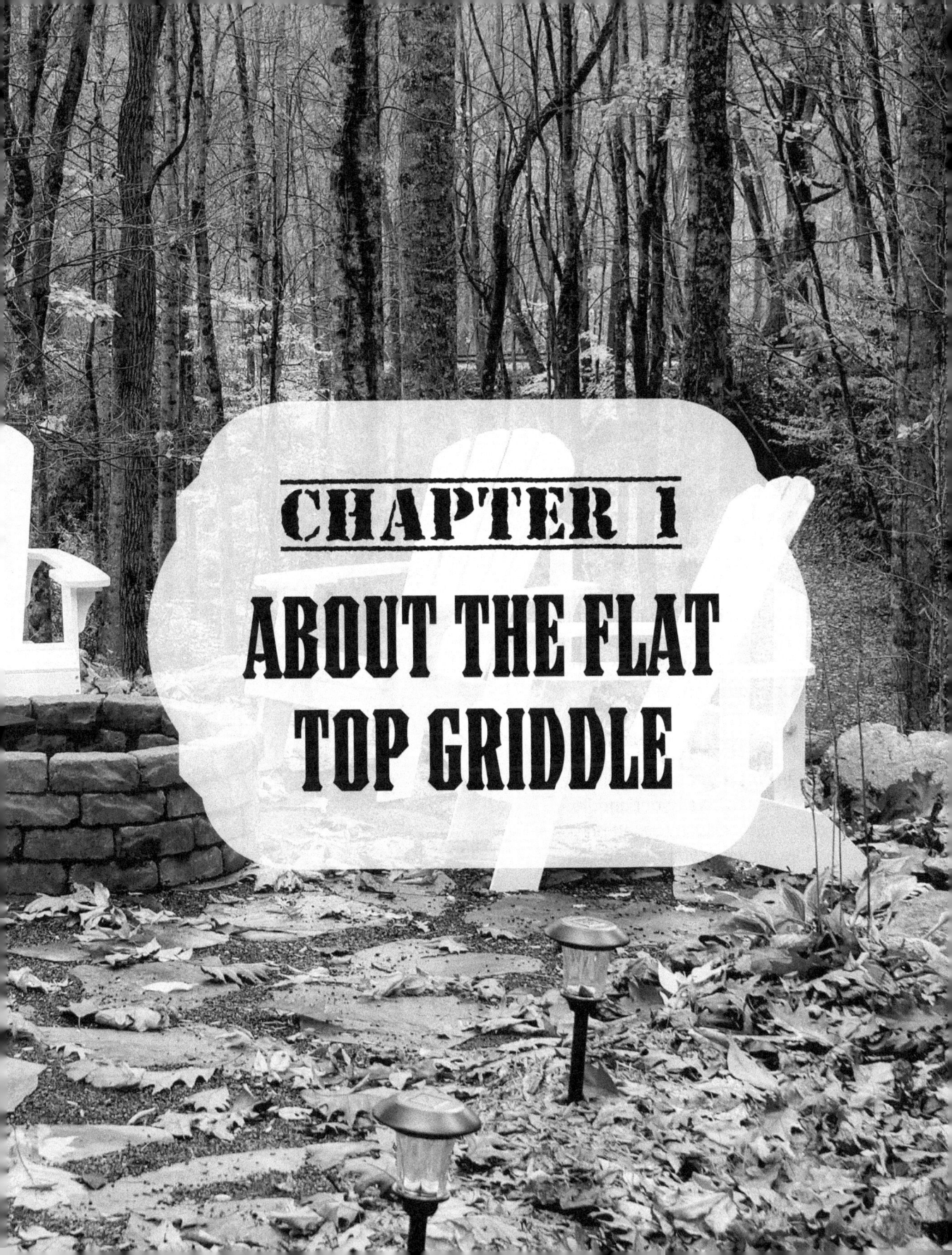

CHAPTER 1
ABOUT THE FLAT TOP GRIDDLE

WHAT DOES IT DO?

Your flat top griddle provides up to 720 inches of professional grade griddle for your back yard or really anywhere you go. Now, you can make professional quality meals and get the same results professional chefs achieve every time you cook. Make eggs, pancakes, quesadillas, grilled cheese, steak, potatoes, teppanyaki style foods and more. The flat top griddle is designed to produce perfectly even and adjustable heat over four different cooking zones, so you can always have the exact temperature you need at a moment's notice.

Your flat top griddle is made with professional grade materials and provides professional quality heat in the form of 60,000 BTU of cooking power with four independent cooking zones. This means you can carefully control everything you cook with individual controls for each zone. Eggs don't cook properly at the same temperature as a steak, and your griddle allows you to cook both, perfectly, at the same time.

Are you an avid camper? Do you love to tailgate before the big game? Do you like to cook at friends' houses? Well, your griddle allows you maximum flexibility by letting you take your griddle wherever you need to go. With minimal effort you can remove the flat top, safely fold and stow the legs, and remove the propane tank. Best of all, the griddle comes with casters so you can roll the griddle wherever it needs to go.

Because it's built from industrial grade materials, your griddle will be a versatile appliance for many years to come. The frame of the griddle is built with super durable powder coated steel. The burners are made from restaurant grade stainless

steel and are guaranteed to produce perfectly even and powerful heat for years to come. Once you've spent some time with your griddle you might even consider getting rid of your more conventional gas or charcoal grills.

Say goodbye to dirty charcoal and matches forever. Charcoal is dirty, expensive, and harmful to your health, so why are you still using it? Your griddle uses a standard refillable propane tank which attaches to the griddle with ease. And thanks to the simple push button ignitor, starting your griddle is as easy as pushing a button.

WHO IS IT GOOD FOR?

Because an outdoor griddle is large enough to cook all the parts of a complete meal at the same time, it is perfect for families who love perfectly prepared backyard favorites like burgers, steaks, and veggies, but it's also perfect for families who love to make big breakfasts. Prepare eggs, bacon, hashbrowns, and pancakes for everyone at the same time.

Do you love to cook big meals on the go? An outdoor Griddle is perfect for camping and tailgating because of how easy it is to transport and set up. Pack it up for your next camping trip and set it up when you want to make an amazing outdoor meal. An outdoor griddle is also perfect for anyone who loves making fresh grilled food for a professional tailgate party. Since your griddle easily fits in the trunk of a car, you can take it with you to the game and set it up in minutes. Impress the whole parking lot with the amazing food you make for your fellow fans.

WHO IS IT NOT GOOD FOR?

Everyone loves food cooked in the open air,

but if you don't have a large enough outdoor space in which to use the griddle, this may not be for you. A good rule of thumb is that you can use the griddle anywhere you would use a conventional gas or charcoal grill.

A FEW CAUTIONS

Because outdoor griddles use an external propane tank, you will want to exercise caution while connecting and disconnecting the tank. Always make sure all connection points are clean and free of debris. When attaching the hose to the tank, make sure the valve is completely tight before allowing gas to flow to the griddle.

Your griddle's cold rolled steel flat top produces amazing results, but because it gets very hot, you should make sure children are always supervised when near the griddle.

WHAT ARE ITS HEALTH BENEFITS?

Charcoal grilling has been the standard for many years, but it carries a whole host of risks. First of all, charcoal fires increase the risk of fires in your yard. That's pretty bad, but did you know that cooking with charcoal also increases your risk of cancer? The combination of charcoal, lighter fluid, and dripping fats causes a variety of compounds that are considered carcinogenic. And you're not just breathing these chemicals when you cook. They're actually coating your food! Charcoal grills also contribute to air pollution by releasing large amounts of carbon monoxide and carbon dioxide into the atmosphere. An outdoor griddle, on the other hand, uses no charcoal and is much safer to use.

A BRIEF HISTORY OF GRILLING

You may not be surprised to hear that grilling food is a pretty old technique. In fact, it goes back over a half a million years. Early humans found that meat cooked over fire was actually more nutritious than raw meat. The reason? Bioavailability. In short, cooking meat changes the structure of proteins and fats allowing them to be more efficiently digested and absorbed by the body. Until the 1940s grilling was mostly something that people did around campfires, but after World War II and the expansion of suburbs, the popularity of backyard grilling skyrocketed. By the 1950s the back yard BBQ was a staple of family entertaining, and it remains this way today.

BETTER THAN CONVENTIONAL GRILLS?

Since the invention of the burger, the debate has raged over whether a grill or a flat top griddle does the best job. While it's true that grills offer burgers a smokier flavor, does that really result in a better burger? After years of research burger experts reached the conclusion that the flat top griddle is actually superior to the grill for one simple reason: It allows the burger to cook in its own juices rather that have all of those juices fall through the grate and into the fire. The end result is a more evenly cooked, juicier, more flavorful burger.

MODERN GAS GRIDDLES

When most people think of griddles they either picture a small counter top griddle that you plug in, or a giant flat top that sits in the kitchen of a diner. Because the griddle is so perfect for cooking such a wide variety of foods, the invention of the modern gas griddle makes perfect sense. By marrying the idea of a propane grill with the cooking surface of a griddle, you get an appliance that is both versatile and portable.

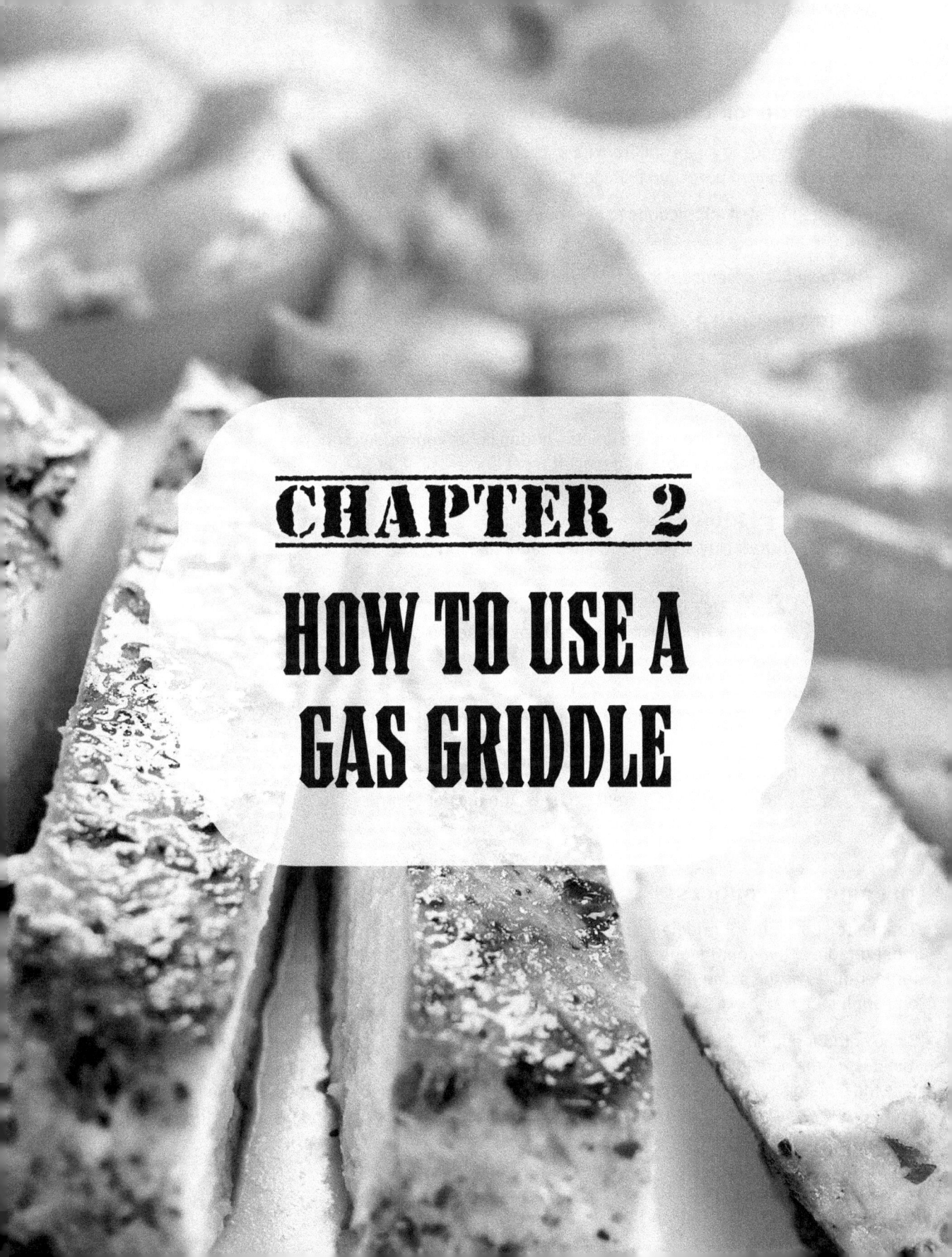

CHAPTER 2
HOW TO USE A GAS GRIDDLE

SETTING UP THE GRIDDLE

Once you have removed a gas grill from its packaging, be sure to consult the user manual to ensure you have all of the included parts and fasteners.

Follow the step-by-step instructions to assemble the griddle, and makes sure to place it on a level surface so that it cannot roll.

Once you have fully assembled the griddle, you can use the valve hose to attach a canister of propane.

LEARNING THE CONTROLS

A gas griddle has easy to use controls that will have you cooking in no time.

1. IGNITION BUTTON:
The battery controlled ignition button lights your griddle. Simply press, hold, and the left most burner will light.

2. LEFT BURNER KNOB:
Turn clockwise to control the heat on the left burner.

3. LEFT-CENTER BURNER KNOB:
Turn clockwise to increase the heat on the left-center burner.

4. RIGHT-CENTER BURNER KNOB:
Turn clockwise to increase the heat on the right-center burner.

5. RIGHT BURNER KNOB:
Turn clockwise to increase the heat on the right burner.

THE GRIDDLING PROCESS

Thanks to your outdoor griddle you can make almost anything with amazing results. Because most griddles have four independent zones, you are free to cook different foods at different temperatures at the same time. Unlike conventional grills, this gives you far greater flexibility with one appliance.

Since outdoor griddles features a heavy cold rolled steel cooking surface, you will need to wait a few minutes for the burners to properly heat the surface. To prevent your food from sticking, you should take the time to season your griddle before use. We'll cover the seasoning process in the Pro Tips section. Once you have finished cooking, turn the burners off one by one, and be sure to turn off the valve on the propane tank.

PERFECT OUTDOOR GAS GRIDDLE

WORKAROUNDS

Your griddle features an easy to use ignition system, but if you find that the ignition burner is not lighting there are several possible causes. First, check to see if the battery in the ignitor has enough power. If that is not the problem, make sure you have enough gas in the tank. Another problem may be a clogged burner or gas jet. Because food or other debris can fall into the burners, they may become clogged over time. If this is the case, remove the cooking surface and use a damp sponge to clean out the burners or gas jets.

Some users have noticed that the grease drain can allow grease to drip out of the trough and down the leg of the grill, which can cause grease to pool on the ground. In order to combat this, make sure the grease trough and the catch can are properly aligned. Misalignment can cause leaks. Also, make sure to monitor the grease level so that it does not overflow or overwhelm the grease drain. Be mindful of bits of food that may fall into the grease trough as these may also cause the grease drain to become clogged.

If you find that food sticks to the surface of the griddle, there are several causes with simple solutions. First, you may not have properly seasoned the griddle. Because the griddle does not come pre-seasoned you should be sure to do this before using. Your food may also stick because you are adding it to the griddle too soon. Since the heavy cooking surface needs a little time to heat up, make sure that it is at the proper temperature before adding food. You can do this by touching a corner or small piece of food to the griddle. If it immediately sticks, wait another few minutes. Another common cause of food sticking to the griddle, is not giving it enough time to cook. Great chefs know that you shouldn't be in a hurry to flip your food. This is because most foods undergo a chemical reaction called the Maillard reaction which creates a charred layer on the food by raising it to a certain temperature. This reaction is also responsible for what is commonly known as a "sear." Giving your food enough time to sear before flipping will ensure it does not stick.

10 Minute Quick-Start

LET'S GET STARTED!

Since your griddle has four individual temperature zones you can cook all the components of a burger at once. This is perfect for camping or for a festive weekend breakfast for the whole family. We're going to start with classic bacon cheese burger. This amazing burger is sure to excite the entire family.

1 COLLECT THESE INGREDIENTS

- 2 lbs. ground chuck
- 4 slices sharp cheddar cheese
- 8 slices bacon
- 4 potato buns
- 1 tomato, sliced
- 1 head iceberg lettuce
- Salt and black pepper

2 COLLECT THESE TOOLS

- Pairing knife
- Instant read thermometer
- Spatula
- Paper towels

The goal of "10 Minute Quick-Start" is to walk you through making your first meal so you "learn by doing" in under 10 minutes. Once you've had a chance to get familiar with how your grill works, you can begin experimenting with all different types of foods.

3 FOLLOW THESE INSTRUCTIONS

1. Light your griddle, and set the right two burners to medium-high and the left two burners to medium heat.

2. Slice the tomatoes and lettuce and set aside.

3. Place the bacon on the medium heat and cook to desired crispiness. Season the burgers with salt and pepper and place on the medium-high heat side.

4. When the burgers have cooked for about five minutes, flip and top with slices of cheese. Remove the bacon from the griddle and drain on the paper towels.

5. When the burgers have cooked an additional four to five minutes, remove them from the griddle and place on the buns. Top with slices of bacon, lettuce, and tomato to serve.

6. And that's it! you've just made your first burger on your outdoor griddle.

CONGRATULATIONS!

You now have a perfectly cooked burgers for the whole family, and you have learned the basics of how to use your outdoor griddle!

CHAPTER 3
PRO TIPS

SEASON THE COOKING SURFACE

Like most high quality cooking appliances, the cold rolled steel cooking surface of your outdoor griddle needs to be properly seasoned to ensure optimal cooking results. So, you may be asking, "what is seasoning?" Before non-stick coatings existed, there was only one way to make sure food didn't stick to the cooking surface. By creating a layer of burnt on oil, you will not only achieve a perfect non-stick surface, you will also protect the cooking surface from scratches and oxidation. Let's get started. First, use soap and water to thoroughly wash the cooking surface. Use a cloth to dry the surface. Next, apply a small amount of oil to the cooking surface. The best oils to use are those with a high smoke point like vegetable or canola. Use a paper towel to spread the oil evenly across the cooking surface. Turn on all four burners and set the temperature to 275°F. Wait until the oil begins to smoke and the surface begins to darken. Once it is smoking, turn off the burners and allow the griddle to cool. Repeat this process two to three more times until the entire surface is evenly dark. Now your griddle is naturally non-stick and protected from damage and rust.

KEEP YOUR GRIDDLE WORKING FROM SEASON TO SEASON

Because you are most likely going to keep your griddle outside, you will need to make sure to do a few things before you store it and before you use it again after being stored. Before you store, make sure to disconnect the gas tank and store away from the griddle with a cap on the valve. You can also purchase a cover for the griddle to keep out insects and dust. When you are ready to start using your griddle again, make sure to check the burner area for spider webs. Webs are flammable and can cause flare ups if you do not clean them out before cooking. Check the level in your gas tank to make sure you have enough fuel to start cooking. Once the tank is attached and you are ready to cook, it's a good idea to perform a new season on the cooking surface. Simply follow the instructions above and your griddle will be good as new.

THE BEST WAY TO CLEAN YOUR GRIDDLE

After each use you will want to clean your griddle, but your griddle should not be cleaned like regular pots and pans. Since you want to build up a nice coating of seasoning to protect your griddle and get the best possible results, you need to make sure not to use things like dish soap to clean the cooking surface. Most detergents have a grease cutting ingredient and this will eat right through your layer of seasoning. The best way to clean your griddle is the way the pros do in restaurants: with a griddle scraper and hot water. You can purchase a griddle scraper which is designed to get rid of any bits of food left behind without sacrificing the seasoning layer you've achieved. To remove things like fat or sauces, a wash with very hot water will dissolve most things, which you can then scrape away. While you don't have to season your grill after every cleaning, continuous seasoning will ensure that your griddle stays dark and shiny.

INVEST IN THE PROPER TOOLS

Since your outdoor griddle is most likely a professional grade piece of equipment, you should have professional grade cooking tools to get the most out of it. While you may have an array of spatulas in the kitchen, to get the best out of your griddle, we recommend buying two long metal spatulas. These spatulas are not only durable, they allow you to transport and flip a large amount of food at the same

time. They are also thin and flexible so you can scoop up things like a whole hash brown without dropping anything. Also recommended are at least one pair of long handled metal tongs which will allow you to reach anywhere on the griddle without worrying about getting burned.

TRY DIFFERENT COOKING FATS

Unlike a traditional grill which allows any cooking fat to fall onto the coals or gas jets, an outdoor flat top griddle keeps your cooking fat right where you want it: on your food! Because of this, you can experiment with different flavors of cooking fat to optimize your results. Different oils impart different flavors, but they also work differently from each other. Olive oil imparts a robust and sometimes spicy black pepper flavor that gives an extra richness to food. The problem with olive oil, however, is that is has a pretty low smoke point, which means that over a certain temperature, the oil will start to taste burned. Use olive oil for foods you are cooking at lower to medium temperature, but avoid it for foods cooked over high heat. If you're looking for oil for high heat cooking, try canola or regular vegetable oil. They will allow you to cook to high heats without that unpleasant burnt taste. And of course, butter packs more flavor than almost anything, but it also has a tendency to burn; so use butter for low heat cooking or for foods you plan to cook quickly.

THE ULTIMATE BURGER

For centuries, mankind has quested after the perfect burger. Since its invention, burger chefs have argued about the best way to grind it; the best way to form the patties; and of course... the best way to cook it. Some say you have to use fancy Wagyu beef imported from Japan, some say the best method is high heat over

charcoal. Well, we're going to put the debate to rest once and for all. The first key to the best burger you've ever had is fat content. If you go to your local supermarket you usually have a choice between 20 percent fat or 10 percent fat. For the perfect burger, this will not do. The perfect burger has between 25 and 30 percent fat, and the best way to achieve this is to grind it yourself using a combination of chuck and short rib. If you don't feel like doing this at home, talk to your local butcher and tell them that you need ground beef with a higher fat content. Also, but sure to always use freshly ground beef. The longer it's sitting in packaging the more compressed it's getting, and compressed beef is the enemy of the perfect burger.

Once you have the right beef, form it into loose balls about 1/3 of a pound. Don't work it too much, and don't press it together, as you want the balls to just barely hold together. Light your griddle and turn the burners to medium heat. You might think that burgers cook best at high heat, but this is wrong. You want to give your burgers time to let their fat render and develop a nice flavorful sear. If you cook too fast you'll end up with overcooked burgers that are chewy inside. Drizzle a little vegetable oil on the griddle and place the ball on the griddle. Using a grill weight, press down to "smash" the burger as flat as you'd like. Don't reshape it, just let it press onto the griddle and sprinkle with salt. Use your thumb to make an indentation in the center of the burger so that it stays flat. When the first side has developed a nice sear, flip, season with salt and cook for an equal amount of time. This way your burger will have the time to render it's fat and reabsorb it as it cooks. When you've reached the temperature you prefer, remove it from the griddle and allow it to rest for five minutes. Top it however you'd like and enjoy what will be the best burger you've ever had.

CHAPTER 4
BREAKFAST

CLASSIC FRENCH TOAST

SERVINGS: 4

Prep time: 5 minutes
Cook time: 10 minutes

INGREDIENTS

6 eggs, beaten

1/4 cup "half and half" or heavy cream

8 slices thick cut white or sourdough bread

2 tablespoons sugar

1 tablespoon cinnamon

1 teaspoon salt

Butter

Powdered sugar

Maple syrup

The perfectly even heat from your outdoor griddle ensures that your French toast comes out evenly cooked and perfectly golden brown.

DIRECTIONS

1. Heat your griddle to medium heat.
2. In a large bowl, combine the eggs, cream, sugar, cinnamon, and salt. Mix well until smooth.
3. Lightly grease the griddle with butter or vegetable oil.
4. Dip each slice of bread in the mixture until well saturated with egg then place onto the griddle.
5. When the French toast has begun to brown, flip and cook until the other side has browned as well. About four minutes.
6. Remove the French toast from the griddle, dust with powdered sugar, and serve with warm maple syrup.

Nutritional Info: Calories: 332, Sodium: 593mg, Dietary Fiber: 2.4g, Fat: 10.5g, Carbs: 44.2g, Protein: 16g.

CLASSIC BUTTERMILK PANCAKES

SERVINGS: 4

Prep time: 5 minutes
Cook time: 10 minutes

While your outdoor griddle is perfect for making all kinds of fun dishes, these buttermilk pancakes will amaze the while family. And thanks to your griddle's even heat, they will come out perfectly golden brown.

INGREDIENTS

2 cups all-purpose flour

3 tablespoons sugar

1-1/2 teaspoons baking powder

1-1/2 teaspoons baking soda

1-1/4 teaspoons salt

2-1/2 cups buttermilk

2 eggs

3 tablespoons unsalted butter, melted

Vegetable oil

DIRECTIONS

1. In a large bowl, combine the flour, sugar, baking soda, baking powder, and salt.
2. Stir in the buttermilk, eggs, and butter, and mix until combined but not totally smooth.
3. Heat your griddle to medium heat and add a small amount of oil. Using a paper towel, spread the oil over the griddle in a very thin layer.
4. Use a ladle to pour the batter onto the griddle allowing a few inches between pancakes.
5. When the surface of the pancakes is bubbly, flip and cook a few additional minutes. Remove the pancakes from the griddle and serve immediately with butter and maple syrup.

Nutritional Info: Calories: 432, Sodium: 458mg, Dietary Fiber: 1.7g, Fat: 12.8g, Carbs: 65.1g, Protein: 14.4g.

FLUFFY BLUEBERRY PANCAKES

SERVINGS: 2

Prep time: 10 minutes
Cook time: 10 minutes

INGREDIENTS

1 cup flour

3/4 cup milk

2 tablespoons white vinegar

2 tablespoons sugar

1 teaspoon baking powder

1/2 teaspoon baking soda

1/2 teaspoon salt

1 egg

2 tablespoons butter, melted

1 cup fresh blueberries

Butter for cooking

These delightful blueberry pancakes use a dash of vinegar to produce the fluffiest most delicious blueberry pancakes you've ever had. Cooking them on your outdoor griddle means you can cook them all evenly, at once!

DIRECTIONS

1. In a bowl, combine the milk and vinegar. Set aside for two minutes.
2. In a large bowl, combine the flour, sugar, baking powder, baking soda, and salt. Stir in the milk, egg, blueberries, and melted butter. Mix until combined but not totally smooth.
3. Heat your griddle to medium heat and add a little butter. Pour the pancakes onto the griddle and cook until one side is golden brown. Flip the pancakes and cook until the other side is golden.
4. Remove the pancakes from the griddle and serve with warm maple syrup.

Nutritional Info: Calories: 499, Sodium: 356mg, Dietary Fiber: 3.5g, Fat: 16.5g, Carbs: 76.2g, Protein: 12.9g.

SIMPLE FRENCH CREPES

SERVINGS: 4

Prep time: 1 hour
Cook time: 15 minutes

INGREDIENTS

- 1-1/4 cups flour
- 3/4 cup whole milk
- 1/2 cup water
- 2 eggs
- 3 tablespoons unsalted butter, melted
- 1 teaspoon vanilla
- 2 tablespoon sugar

The great thing about these delicate and traditional crepes is they can be made either sweet or savory. The even heat provided by your outdoor griddle ensures that all of your crepes come out perfectly even.

DIRECTIONS

1. In a large bowl, add all the ingredients and mix with a whisk. Make sure the batter is smooth. Rest for 1 hour.
2. Heat your griddle to medium heat and add a thin layer of butter. Add about ¼ cup of the batter. Using a crepe spreading tool, form your crepe and cook for 1-2 minutes. Use your Crepe Spatula and flip. Cook for another minute.
3. Top with Nutella and strawberries for a sweet crepe, or top with scrambled eggs and black forest ham for a savory crepe

Nutritional Info: Calories: 303, Sodium: 112mg, Dietary Fiber: 1.1g, Fat: 12.7g, Carbs: 38.2g, Protein: 8.4g.

CLASSIC DENVER OMELETTE

SERVINGS: 2

Prep time: 5 minutes
Cook time: 10 minutes

INGREDIENTS

6 large eggs

1/4 cup country ham, diced

1/4 cup yellow onion, finely chopped

1/4 cup green bell pepper, chopped

2/3 cup cheddar cheese, shredded

1/4 teaspoon cayenne pepper

Salt and black pepper

2 tablespoons butter

Perhaps one of the most famous omelettes of all time, the Denver Omelette is a classic because it brings together timeless flavors for a dish that just screams breakfast.

DIRECTIONS

1. Heat your griddle to medium heat and place the butter onto the griddle.
2. Add the ham, onion, and pepper to the butter and cook until the vegetables have just softened.
3. Beat the eggs in a large bowl and add a pinch of salt and the cayenne pepper.
4. Split the vegetables into to portions on the griddle and add half of the eggs to each portion. Cook until the eggs have begun to firm up, and then add the cheese to each omelet.
5. Fold the omelets over and remove from the griddle. Serve immediately.

Nutritional Info: Calories: 507, Sodium: 747mg, Dietary Fiber: 0.8g, Fat: 40.5g, Carbs: 4.9g, Protein: 31.5g.

BACON AND GRUYERE OMELETTE

SERVINGS: 2

Prep Time: 5 minutes
Cook Time: 15 minutes

INGREDIENTS

6 eggs, beaten

6 strips bacon

1/4 lb gruyere, shredded

1 teaspoon black pepper

1 teaspoon salt

1 tablespoon chives, finely chopped

Vegetable oil

The combination of smoky bacon and rich gruyere cheese pairs perfectly with delicately cooked eggs. If you don't have any gruyere on hand, you can substitute sharp cheddar.

DIRECTIONS

1. Add salt to the beaten eggs and set aside for 10 minutes.
2. Heat your griddle to medium heat and add the bacon strips. Cook until most of the fat has rendered, but bacon is still flexible. Remove the bacon from the griddle and place on paper towels.
3. Once the bacon has drained, chop into small pieces.
4. Add the eggs to the griddle in two even pools. Cook until the bottom of the eggs starts to firm up. Add the gruyere to the eggs and cook until the cheese has started to melt and the eggs are just starting to brown.
5. Add the bacon pieces and use a spatula to turn one half of the omelette onto the other half. Remove from the griddle, season with pepper and chives and serve.

Nutritional Info: Calories: 734, Sodium: 855mg, Dietary Fiber: 0.3g, Fat: 55.3g, Carbs: 2.8g, Protein: 54.8g.

BACON EGG AND CHEESE SANDWICH

SERVINGS: 4

Prep time: 5 minutes
Cook time: 10 minutes

INGREDIENTS

4 large eggs

8 strips of bacon

4 slices cheddar or American cheese

8 slices sourdough bread

2 tablespoons butter

2 tablespoons vegetable oil

A classic sandwich that is great for breakfast or any time of the day. Your outdoor griddle allows you to make every component of this sandwich at once, with ease.

DIRECTIONS

1. Heat your griddle to medium heat and place the strips of bacon on one side. Cook until just slightly crispy.
2. When the bacon is nearly finished, place the oil on the other side of the griddle and crack with eggs onto the griddle. Cook them either sunny side up or over medium.
3. Butter one side of each slice of bread and place them butter side down on the griddle. Place a slice of cheese on 4 of the slices of bread and when the cheese has just started to melt and the eggs are finished, stack the eggs on the bread.
4. Add the bacon to the sandwiches and place the other slice of bread on top. Serve immediately.

Nutritional Info: Calories: 699, Sodium: 1148mg, Dietary Fiber: 1.5g, Fat: 47.7g, Carbs: 37.8g, Protein: 29.3g.

SAUSAGE AND VEGETABLE SCRAMBLE

SERVINGS: 4

Prep time: 10 minutes
Cook time: 20 minutes

INGREDIENTS

8 eggs, beaten

1/2 lb sausage, sliced into thin rounds or chopped

1 green bell pepper, sliced

1 yellow onion, sliced

1 cup white mushrooms, sliced

1 teaspoon salt

1/2 teaspoon black pepper

Vegetable oil

If you're looking for a fun and easy way to feed the whole family, this delicious egg scramble is sure to please. And it will cook perfectly and quickly on your outdoor griddle.

DIRECTIONS

1. Preheat the griddle to medium-high heat.
2. Brush the griddle with vegetable oil and add the peppers and mushrooms. Cook until lightly browned and then add the onions. Season with salt and pepper and cook until the onions are soft.
3. Add the sausage to the griddle and mix with the vegetables. Cook until lightly browned.
4. Add the eggs and mix with the vegetables and cook until eggs reach desired doneness. Use a large spatula to remove the scramble from the griddle and serve immediately.

Nutritional Info: Calories: 342, Sodium: 1131mg, Dietary Fiber: 1.2g, Fat: 24.9g, Carbs: 6.3g, Protein: 23.2g.

CLASSIC STEAK AND EGGS

SERVINGS: 4

Prep time: 10 minutes
Cook time: 10 minutes

INGREDIENTS

1 pound Sirloin, cut into 4-1/2-inch thick pieces

8 large eggs

3 tablespoons vegetable oil

Salt and black pepper

An old-time breakfast favorite that is sure to start your day right, this steak and eggs recipe is cooked best on your outdoor griddle.

DIRECTIONS

1. Preheat griddle to medium-high heat on one side and medium heat on the other.
2. Season the steaks with a generous amount of salt and pepper.
3. Place steaks on the medium high side and cook for 3 minutes and add the oil to the medium heat side.
4. Flip the steaks and crack the eggs onto the medium heat side of the griddle.
5. After 3 minutes remove the steaks from the griddle and allow to rest 5 minutes. Finish cooking the eggs and place two eggs and one piece of steak on each plate to serve. Season the eggs with a pinch of salt and pepper.

Nutritional Info: Calories: 444, Sodium: 215mg, Dietary Fiber: 0g, Fat: 27.2g, Carbs: 0.8g, Protein: 47g.

TOAD IN A HOLE

SERVINGS: 4

Prep time: 10 minutes
Cook time: 5 minutes

INGREDIENTS

4 slices white, wheat, or sourdough bread

4 eggs

2 tablespoons butter

Salt and black pepper

This classic, simple dish is fun and easy to make. It's sure to delight the kids.

DIRECTIONS

1. Preheat griddle to medium heat add the butter, spreading it around.
2. Cut a hole in the center of each slice of bread.
3. Place the slices of bread on the griddle and crack an egg into the holes in each slice of bread.
4. Cook until the bread begins to brown, then flip and cook until the egg whites are firm.
5. Remove from the griddle and season with salt and black pepper before serving.

Nutritional Info: Calories: 206, Sodium: 311mg, Dietary Fiber: 0.8g, Fat: 10.7g, Carbs: 18.4g, Protein: 9.4g.

ULTIMATE BREAKFAST BURRITO

SERVINGS: 2

Prep time: 5 minutes
Cook time: 20 minutes

INGREDIENTS

4 eggs

4 strips bacon

1 large russet potato, peeled and cut into small cubes

1 red bell pepper

1/2 yellow onion

1 ripe avocado, sliced

2 tablespoon hot sauce

2 large flour tortillas

Vegetable oil

The great thing about your outdoor griddle is that you can cook different things at the same time. This delicious breakfast burrito combines savory flavors for a breakfast the whole family will beg for.

DIRECTIONS

1. Preheat the griddle to medium-high heat on one side and medium heat on the other side. Brush with vegetable oil and add the bacon to the medium heat side and peppers and onions to the medium-high side.

2. When the bacon finishes cooking, place on paper towels and chop into small pieces. Add the potatoes to the bacon fat on the griddle. Cook the potatoes until softened.

3. Add the eggs to the vegetable side and cook until firm. Place the ingredients onto the tortillas and top with slices of avocado and a tablespoon of hot sauce. Fold the tortillas and enjoy.

Nutritional Info: Calories: 793, Sodium: 1800mg, Dietary Fiber: 10.7g, Fat: 41.3.g, Carbs: 73.4g, Protein: 35.8g.

MEXICAN SCRAMBLE

SERVINGS: 4

Prep time: 5 minutes
Cook time: 10 minutes

INGREDIENTS

8 eggs, beaten
1 lb Chorizo
1/2 yellow onion
1 cup cooked black beans
1/2 cup green chilies
1/2 cup jack cheese
1/4 cup green onion, chopped
1/2 teaspoon black pepper
Vegetable oil

This slightly spicy Mexican egg scramble is easy to make and sure to be a hit with friends and family.

DIRECTIONS

1. Preheat a griddle to medium heat. Brush the griddle with vegetable oil and add the chorizo to one side and the onions to the other side.
2. When the onion has softened, combine it with the chorizo and add the beans and chilies.
3. Add the eggs, cheese, and green onion and cook until eggs have reached desired firmness.
4. Remove the scramble from the griddle and season with black pepper before serving.

Nutritional Info: Calories: 843, Sodium: 1554mg, Dietary Fiber: 9.2g, Fat: 54.1g, Carbs: 38.2g, Protein: 50.7g.

HASH BROWN SCRAMBLE

SERVINGS: 4

Prep time: 10 minutes
Cook time: 10 minutes

INGREDIENTS

2 russet potatoes, shredded, rinsed, and drained

8 eggs, beaten

1 cup cheddar cheese

6 slices bacon, cut into small pieces

1/3 cup green onion, chopped

Vegetable oil

This fun dish is easy to make and combines all of your favorite breakfast items into one hearty scramble.

DIRECTIONS

1. Preheat griddle to medium heat and brush with vegetable oil.

2. On one side, place the potatoes on the griddle and spread in a 1/2 inch thick layer. Cook the potatoes until golden brown and then flip. Add the bacon to the other side of the griddle and cook until the fat has rendered.

3. Add the eggs and cheese to the top of the hash browns and stir in the bacon and green onion. Cook until the cheese has melted and divide equally among 4 plates.

Nutritional Info: Calories: 470, Sodium: 965mg, Dietary Fiber: 2.8g, Fat: 30.2g, Carbs: 18.8g, Protein: 30.6g.

GOLDEN HASH BROWNS

SERVINGS: 4

Prep time: 10 minutes
Cook time: 15 minutes

INGREDIENTS

3 russet potatoes, peeled
1 tablespoon onion powder
1 tablespoon salt
1 teaspoon black pepper
Vegetable oil

This classic breakfast side is cooked to perfect golden brown perfection on your outdoor griddle. Pair them with eggs, pancakes, or really anything for a delicious breakfast.

DIRECTIONS

1. Using the largest holes on a box grater, grate the potatoes and place in a large bowl. When all of the potatoes have been grated, rinse with water.
2. Squeeze as much water out of the potatoes as possible and return to the bowl.
3. Add the onion powder, salt, and pepper to the bowl and stir to combine.
4. Preheat your griddle to medium heat and add a think layer of oil. Spread the potato mixture onto the grill creating a layer about 1/2 inch thick. Cook for approximately 8 minutes.
5. Working in sections using a large spatula, turn the potatoes and cook an additional 5 to 8 minutes or until both sides are golden brown.
6. Remove the potatoes from the griddle in sections and add to plates. Sprinkle with a pinch of salt and serve immediately.

Nutritional Info: Calories: 118, Sodium: 1755mg, Dietary Fiber: 4.1g, Fat: 0.2g, Carbs: 26.8g, Protein: 2.9g.

POTATO BACON HASH

SERVINGS: 6 - 8

Prep time: 30 minutes
Cook time: 3 hours

INGREDIENTS

6 slices thick cut bacon

2 russet potatoes, cut into 1/2 inch chunks

1 yellow onion, chopped

1 red bell pepper, chopped

1 clove garlic, finely chopped

1 teaspoon salt

1/2 teaspoon black pepper

1 tablespoon Tabasco sauce

Perfect for a hearty breakfast or as a robust side dish, this bacon and potato hash is perfect for all occasions and your outdoor griddle ensures that it comes out evenly cooked and delicious.

DIRECTIONS

1. Set your griddle to medium heat and cook the bacon until just crispy.

2. Add the potato, onion, and bell pepper to the griddle and cook until the potato has softened. Use the large surface of the griddle to spread out the ingredients.

3. When the potato has softened, add the garlic, salt, and pepper.

4. Chop the bacon into small pieces and add it to the griddle. Stir the mixture well and add the hot sauce right before removing the hash from the griddle. Serve immediately.

Nutritional Info: Calories: 154, Sodium: 475mg, Dietary Fiber: 1.8g, Fat: 10.2g, Carbs: 11.3g, Protein: 4.5g.

CHAPTER 5
SANDWICHES & BREADS

TANGY CHICKEN SANDWICHES

SERVINGS: 4

Prep time: 30 minutes
Cook time: 20 minutes

INGREDIENTS

2 lbs. chicken breast, sliced into 4 cutlets

4 potato buns, toasted

FOR THE MARINADE:

1/2 cup pickle juice

1 tablespoon Dijon mustard

1 teaspoon paprika

1/2 teaspoon black pepper

1/2 teaspoon salt

The bright tangy flavor of pickle juice is the perfect way to create a fresh and flavorful marinade for chicken sandwiches!

DIRECTIONS

1. Mix marinade ingredients together in a mixing bowl.
2. Place chicken in marinade and marinate for 30 minutes in the refrigerator.
3. Preheat griddle to medium-high. Wipe off extra marinade and sear chicken for 7 minutes per side, or until a meat thermometer reaches 165°F.
4. Allow chicken to rest for 5 minutes after grilling and serve on toasted buns.

Nutritional Info: Calories: 265, Sodium: 685mg, Dietary Fiber: 0.6g, Fat: 6g, Carbs: 1.1g, Protein: 48.4g.

SAVORY CHICKEN BURGERS

SERVINGS: 3

Prep time: 10 minutes
Cook time: 20 minutes

INGREDIENTS

1 lb. ground chicken

1/2 red onion, finely chopped

1 teaspoon garlic powder

1/2 teaspoon onion powder

1/4 teaspoon black pepper

1/2 teaspoon salt

3 tablespoons vegetable oil

3 potato buns, toasted

If you're looking for a great alternative to traditional beef burgers, these chicken burgers are lighter and packed with flavor.

DIRECTIONS

1. In a large bowl, combine the ground chicken, onion, garlic powder, onion powder, pepper, and salt. Mix well to combine. Form the chicken mixture into three equal patties. Don't work the mixture too much or the burgers will be too dense.

2. Heat your griddle to medium-high heat. Add the vegetable oil.

3. When the oil is shimmering, add the chicken patties and cook 5 minutes per side, or until the patties reach 165°F.

4. Remove the patties from the griddle and allow to rest for five minutes before serving on the toasted buns.

Nutritional Info: Calories: 420, Sodium: 519mg, Dietary Fiber: 0.6g, Fat: 24.8g, Carbs: 2.8g, Protein: 44.2g.

SUN-DRIED TOMATO AND CHICKEN FLATBREADS

SERVINGS: 4

Prep time: 5 minutes
Cook time: 7 minutes

INGREDIENTS

4 flat breads or thin pita bread

FOR THE TOPPING:

1-1/2 cups of sliced grilled chicken, pre-cooked or leftovers

1/2 cup sun-dried tomatoes, coarsely chopped

6 leaves fresh basil, coarsely chopped

3 cups mozzarella cheese, shredded

1 teaspoon salt

1 teaspoon ground black pepper

1 teaspoon red pepper flakes

Olive or chili oil, for serving

Grilled chicken flatbreads are a perfect afternoon snack or lunch option. Serve with a salad for a full meal or enjoy as – is with friends and family on a sunny afternoon. Delicious paired with sparkling water.

DIRECTIONS

1. Preheat the griddle to low heat.
2. Mix all the topping ingredients together in a large mixing bowl with a rubber spatula.
3. Lay flatbreads on griddle, and top with an even amount of topping mixture; spreading to the edges of each.
4. Tent the flatbreads with foil for 5 minutes each, or until cheese is just melted.
5. Place flatbreads on a flat surface or cutting board, and cut each with a pizza cutter or kitchen scissors.
6. Drizzle with olive or chili oil to serve!

Nutritional Info: Calories: 276, Sodium: 1061mg, Dietary Fiber: 1.9g, Fat: 5.7g, Carbs: 35.7g, Protein: 19.8g.

TURKEY PESTO PANINI

SERVINGS: 2

Prep time: 5 minutes
Cook time: 6 minutes

INGREDIENTS

1 tablespoon olive oil

4 slices French bread

1/2 cup pesto sauce

4 slices mozzarella cheese

2 cups chopped leftover turkey

1 Roma tomato, thinly sliced

1 avocado, halved, seeded, peeled and sliced

Turkey Pesto Paninis are the perfect quick sandwich to whip up when you are pressed for time. This recipe is delicious served with any soup or salad for one hearty weekday meal or something fun on the weekends.

DIRECTIONS

1. Preheat griddle to medium-high heat.
2. Brush each slice of bread with olive oil on one side.
3. Place 2 slices olive oil side down on the griddle.
4. Spread 2 tablespoons pesto over 1 side of French bread.
5. Top with one slice mozzarella, turkey, tomatoes, avocado, a second slice of mozzarella, and top with second half of bread to make a sandwich; repeat with remaining slices of bread.
6. Cook until the bread is golden and the cheese is melted, about 2-3 minutes per side.
7. Serve warm with your favorite salad or soup.

Nutritional Info: Calories: 1129, Sodium: 1243mg, Dietary Fiber: 10g, Fat: 70.9g, Carbs: 53.2g, Protein: 73g.

CLASSIC AMERICAN BURGER

SERVINGS: 6

Prep time: 15 minutes
Cook time: 35 minutes

INGREDIENTS

2 lbs. ground beef, at least 20% fat

Kosher salt

Black pepper

1 tomato, sliced

1 yellow or red onion, sliced

1 head iceberg lettuce, cut into flats

6 thick pieces of American or medium cheddar cheese

6 seeded buns or potato buns, toasted

The all-time American classic. And probably the best way to cook a burger according to the experts. Your outdoor griddle makes the best burgers you've ever tasted.

DIRECTIONS

1. Divide the ground beef into 6 equal loosely formed balls. Press the balls on a flat surface to make patties. Do not over work them.
2. Generously season the patties with salt and black pepper.
3. Heat your griddle to medium-high heat.
4. Place the patties on the griddle and press down to ensure that the surface makes contact. Cook for three to four minutes.
5. Flip the patties and top with cheese. Cook an additional three to four minutes. The cheese should melt by then.
6. Remove the burgers from the griddle and place them on the buns. Top with lettuce, tomato, and onion, as well as your favorite condiments.

Nutritional Info: Calories: 410, Sodium: 305mg, Dietary Fiber: 0.9g, Fat: 18.8g, Carbs: 4.1g, Protein: 53.4g.

LAYERED BEEF & CORN BURGER

SERVINGS: 6

Prep time: 20 minutes
Cook time: 30 minutes

INGREDIENTS

1 large egg, lightly beaten
1 cup whole kernel corn, cooked
1/2 cup bread crumbs
2 tablespoons shallots, minced
1 teaspoon Worcestershire sauce
2 pounds ground beef
1 teaspoon salt
1/2 teaspoon pepper
1/2 teaspoon ground sage

Whip up something different for dinner with this hearty Corn burger!

DIRECTIONS

1. Combine the egg, corn, bread crumbs, shallots, and Worcestershire sauce in a mixing bowl and set aside.
2. Combine ground beef and seasonings in a separate bowl.
3. Line a flat surface with waxed paper.
4. Roll beef mixture into 12 thin burger patties.
5. Spoon corn mixture into the center of 6 patties and spread evenly across within an inch of the edge.
6. Top each with a second circle of meat and press edges to seal corn mixture in the middle of each burger.
7. Grill over medium heat, for 12-15 minutes on each side or until thermometer reads 160°F and juices run clear.

Nutritional Info: Calories: 354, Sodium: 578mg, Dietary Fiber: 1.2g, Fat: 11.1g, Carbs: 12.3g, Protein: 49.1g.

CHEESY HAM AND PINEAPPLE SANDWICH

SERVINGS: 4

Prep time: 10 minutes
Cook time: 20 minutes

INGREDIENTS

1 (10 ounce) package deli sliced ham

4 pineapple rings

4 slices swiss cheese

8 slices of thick bread

Butter, softened, for brushing

Ooey, gooey cheese meets sweet pineapple and ham for one delicious sandwich. Fix these up for a lunch time treat or double the recipe for a family get together for easy fun food to serve on the weekends.

DIRECTIONS

1. Butter one side of all the slices of bread and heat your griddle to medium heat.
2. On top of each piece of bread, stack 1/4 of the ham, a pineapple ring, and 1 slice of cheese.
3. Place the sandwiches on the griddle and top with another slice of bread.
4. Cook until the bottom bread is golden brown, then flip and cook until the other side of the bread is browned and the cheese is melted.

Nutritional Info: Calories: 594, Sodium: 3184mg, Dietary Fiber: 0.3g, Fat: 40.3g, Carbs: 4.7g, Protein: 47.7g.

CROQUE MADAME

SERVINGS: 2

Prep time: 10 minutes
Cook time: 10 minutes

INGREDIENTS

5 tablespoons butter
1 tablespoon flour
2/3 cup milk
4 slices thick cut bread
4 slices black forest ham
4 slices gruyere cheese
Salt and black pepper
2 eggs

A classic French bistro sandwich which combines a heart bechamel sauce with smoky gruyere for a satisfying lunch or dinner.

DIRECTIONS

1. In a small saucepan over medium heat, melt one tablespoon of butter and add the flour. Whisk until just browned and add the milk. Stir until the sauce has thickened. Remove from heat and season with salt and pepper.

2. Heat your griddle to medium heat. Butter one side of each slice of bread and add a generous amount of the bechamel sauce to the other side.

3. Place two slices of ham on top of each sandwich and top with the other slice of bread. Place on the griddle and cook until golden brown. Flip the sandwiches and top with the gruyere cheese. On the other side of the griddle, crack the eggs and cook until the whites are firm.

4. Cook until the other side of the sandwich is golden brown and the gruyere has melted on top. Top each sandwich with a fried egg before serving.

Nutritional Info: Calories: 538, Sodium: 1019mg, Dietary Fiber: 2.4g, Fat: 35.2g, Carbs: 17.8g, Protein: 36.9g.

SALMON BURGERS

SERVINGS: 4

Prep time: 10 minutes
Cook time: 15 minutes

INGREDIENTS

4 potato buns
2 lbs salmon, finely chopped
1/2 red onion, finely chopped
1 stalk celery, finely chopped
1/2 teaspoon garlic powder
2 teaspoons Dijon mustard
1 teaspoon salt
4 slices tomato
2 tablespoons vegetable oil

These savory and delicious salmon burgers are an amazing alternative to traditional burgers and they cook to perfection on your outdoor griddle.

DIRECTIONS

1. In a large bowl, combine the chopped salmon, onion, celery, garlic powder, mustard, and salt. Mix well and form into 4 equal patties.

2. Heat your griddle to medium heat and add the vegetable oil. When oil is shimmering add the salmon patties, cooking 6 to 7 minutes per side. Remove from the griddle, place on the buns and top with sliced tomato to serve.

Nutritional Info: Calories: 512, Sodium: 935mg, Dietary Fiber: 3.7g, Fat: 22.5g, Carbs: 32.4g, Protein: 49.5g.

ULTIMATE GRILLED CHEESE

SERVINGS: 4

Prep time: 10 minutes
Cook time: 10 minutes

INGREDIENTS

- 8 slices sourdough bread
- 4 slices provolone cheese
- 4 slices yellow American cheese
- 4 slices sharp cheddar cheese
- 4 slices tomato
- 3 tablespoons mayonnaise
- 3 tablespoons butter

This updated take on grilled cheese takes the classic sandwich to the next level. Combining different cheeses creates texture and flavor that is truly mind blowing, and your outdoor griddle ensures perfect results.

DIRECTIONS

1. Heat your griddle to medium heat.
2. Butter one side of each piece of bread and spread mayo on the other side.
3. Place the buttered side down on the griddle and stack the cheeses on top.
4. Place the other pieces of bread, butter side up on top of the cheese and cook until golden brown. Flip and cook until the other piece of bread is golden brown as well and the cheese is melted.
5. Remove from the griddle, slice in half and enjoy.

Nutritional Info: Calories: 521, Sodium: 1044mg, Dietary Fiber: 1.7g, Fat: 30.1g, Carbs: 41.4g, Protein: 22g.

GARLIC PARMESAN GRILLED CHEESE SANDWICHES

SERVINGS: 1

Prep time: 2 minutes
Cook time: 7 minutes

INGREDIENTS

2 slices Italian bread, sliced thin

2 slices provolone cheese

2 tablespoons butter, softened

Garlic powder, for dusting

Dried parsley, for dusting

Parmesan Cheese, shredded, for dusting

Give your grilled cheese a gourmet twist when you elevate them with tangy parmesan cheese. This is my favorite way to enjoy a big bowl of tomato soup or grilled salad found in the recipes above.

DIRECTIONS

1. Spread butter evenly across 2 slices of bread and sprinkle each buttered side with garlic and parsley.
2. Sprinkle a few tablespoons of Parmesan cheese over each buttered side of bread and gently press the cheese into the bread.
3. Preheat the griddle to medium heat and place one slice of bread, buttered side down, into the skillet.
4. Top with provolone slices and second slice of bread with the butter side up.
5. Cook 3 minutes, and flip to cook 3 minutes on the other side; cook until bread is golden and parmesan cheese is crispy.
6. Serve warm with your favorite sides!

Nutritional Info: Calories: 575, Sodium: 1065mg, Dietary Fiber: 2.8g, Fat: 45.1g, Carbs: 18.1g, Protein: 27.6g.

GRILLED PIZZA CHEESE

SERVINGS: 4

Prep Time: 10 minutes
Cook Time: 20 minutes

INGREDIENTS

8 slices French bread
3 tablespoons butter, softened
1/2 cup pizza sauce
1/4 cup mozzarella cheese
1/2 cup pepperoni diced
Garlic powder, for dusting
Oregano, for dusting

Pizza lovers rejoice! You can whip up quick and easy Pizza Grilled Cheese on your outdoor griddle for the whole family in no time.

DIRECTIONS

1. Spread butter on one side of each French bread slice.
2. Place butter side down on a piece of aluminum foil and dust with garlic powder and oregano.
3. Spread pizza sauce on opposite side of all French bread slices.
4. Top 4 slices of bread with mozzarella cheese, a few slices of pepperoni, and additional mozzarella.
5. Place remaining French bread slices on top of pizza topped bread, butter side up, to create 4 sandwiches.
6. Preheat the griddle to medium heat and place one slice of bread, buttered side down into the skillet.
7. Cook, 3 minutes and flip to cook 3 minutes on the other side; cook until bread is golden and cheese is melted.
8. Serve warm and enjoy!

Nutritional Info: Calories: 305, Sodium: 664mg, Dietary Fiber: 2.3g, Fat: 12g, Carbs: 40.4g, Protein: 9.4g.

MINI PORTOBELLO BURGERS

SERVINGS: 4

Prep time: 15 minutes
Cook time: 15 minutes

INGREDIENTS

4 portobello mushroom caps
4 slices mozzarella cheese
4 buns, like brioche

FOR THE MARINADE:

1/4 cup balsamic vinegar
2 tablespoons olive oil
1 teaspoon dried basil
1 teaspoon dried oregano
1 teaspoon garlic powder
1/4 teaspoon sea salt
1/4 teaspoon black pepper

Delicious and nutritious, these Mini Portobello Burgers are a great animal protein alternative and wonderful for those wanting to add veggies to their healthy lifestyle. Simple and easy, serve them with a side of turnip fries or sweet potato fries for a low-calorie meal.

DIRECTIONS

1. Whisk together marinade ingredients in a large mixing bowl. Add mushroom caps and toss to coat.
2. Let stand at room temperature for 15 minutes, turning twice.
3. Preheat griddle for medium-high heat.
4. Place mushrooms on the griddle; reserve marinade for basting.
5. Cook for 5 to 8 minutes on each side, or until tender.
6. Brush with marinade frequently.
7. Top with mozzarella cheese during the last 2 minutes of cooking.
8. Remove from griddle and serve on brioche buns.

Nutritional Info: Calories: 248, Sodium: 429mg, Dietary Fiber: 2.1g, Fat: 13.5g, Carbs: 20.3g, Protein: 13g.

VEGGIE PESTO FLATBREAD

SERVINGS: 4

Prep time: 40 minutes
Cook time: 10 minutes

INGREDIENTS

2 prepared flatbreads

1 jar pesto

1 cup shredded mozzarella cheese

FOR THE TOPPING:

1/2 cup cherry tomatoes, halved

1 small red onion, sliced thin

1 red bell pepper, sliced

1 yellow bell pepper, sliced

1/2 cup mixed black and green olives, halved

1 small yellow squash or zucchini, sliced

2 teaspoon olive oil

1/4 teaspoon sea salt

1/4 teaspoon black pepper

Grilled Veggie Pesto Flatbreads are simply perfect for any weekend or party with family and friends. When it comes to having vegetarian options for everybody, this is a great way to create a special sharing flatbread so everyone is included in the grilling fun.

DIRECTIONS

1. Preheat the griddle to low heat.
2. Spread an even amount of pesto onto each flatbread.
3. Top with 1/2 cup mozzarella cheese each.
4. Mix all the topping ingredients together in a large mixing bowl with a rubber spatula.
5. Lay flatbreads on griddle, and top with an even amount of topping mixture; spreading to the edges of each.
6. Tent the flatbreads with foil for 5 minutes each, or until cheese is just melted.
7. Place flatbreads on a flat surface or cutting board, and cut each with a pizza cutter or kitchen scissors.
8. Serve warm!

Nutritional Info: Calories: 177, Sodium: 482mg, Dietary Fiber: 1.7g, Fat: 11.9g, Carbs: 12.6g, Protein: 5.5g.

GRILLED VEGETABLE PIZZA

SERVINGS: 6

Prep time: 30 minutes
Cook time: 10 minutes

INGREDIENTS

8 small fresh mushrooms, halved

1 small zucchini, cut into 1/4-inch slices

1 small yellow pepper, sliced

1 small red pepper, sliced

1 small red onion, sliced

1 tablespoon white wine vinegar

1 tablespoon water

4 teaspoons olive oil, divided

1/2 teaspoon dried basil

1/4 teaspoon sea salt

1/4 teaspoon pepper

1 prebaked, 12-inch thin whole wheat pizza crust

1 can (8 ounces) pizza sauce

2 small tomatoes, chopped

2 cups shredded part-skim mozzarella cheese

Grilled Vegetable Pizzas are a great weeknight treat or a way to use the summer vegetables in your garden. Just be sure to get creative with your toppings and you'll really savor this delicious grilled pizza.

DIRECTIONS

1. Preheat your griddle to medium-high heat.
2. Combine mushrooms, zucchini, peppers, onion, vinegar, water, 3 teaspoons oil and seasonings in a large mixing bowl.
3. Transfer to griddle and cook over medium heat for 10 minutes or until tender, stirring often.
4. Brush crust with remaining oil and spread with pizza sauce.
5. Top evenly with grilled vegetables, tomatoes and cheese.
6. Tent with aluminum foil and griddle over medium heat for 5 to 7 minutes or until edges are lightly browned and cheese is melted.
7. Serve warm!

Nutritional Info: Calories: 111, Sodium: 257mg, Dietary Fiber: 1.7g, Fat: 5.4g, Carbs: 12.2g, Protein: 5g.

BACON JALAPENO WRAPS

SERVINGS: 4

Prep time: 5 minutes
Cook time: 10 minutes

INGREDIENTS

1 package bacon, uncured and nitrate free

6 fresh jalapeno peppers, halved lengthwise and seeded

1 (8 ounce) package cream cheese

1 dozen toothpicks, soaked

When bacon meets jalapeno you have a flavor explosion from out of this world! Serve these delicious spicy wraps at your next family get together or tailgate party with cool veggies like carrot and celery sticks on the side.

DIRECTIONS

1. Preheat your griddle to high heat.
2. Fill jalapeno halves with cream cheese.
3. Wrap each with bacon. Secure with a toothpick.
4. Place on the griddle, and cook until bacon is crispy, about 5 to 7 minutes per side.
5. Remove to a platter to cool and serve warm.

Nutritional Info: Calories: 379, Sodium: 1453mg, Dietary Fiber: 0.9g, Fat: 33.4g, Carbs: 3.5g, Protein: 16.3g.

CHAPTER 6
MAIN DISHES: POULTRY

CLASSIC BBQ CHICKEN

SERVINGS: 4 - 6

Prep time: 5 minutes
Cook time: 1 hour 45 minutes

INGREDIENTS

4 pounds of your favorite chicken, including legs, thighs, wings, and breasts, skin-on

Salt

Olive oil

1 cup barbecue sauce, like Hickory Mesquite or homemade

BBQ Chicken has never tasted so good! We love this classic BBQ favorite for a taste of summer all year around. Simply serve with your favorite side dishes for a full family style meal.

DIRECTIONS

1. Rub the chicken with olive oil and salt.
2. Preheat the griddle to high heat.
3. Sear chicken skin side down on the grill for 5-10 minutes.
4. Turn the griddle down to medium low heat, tent with foil and cook for 30 minutes.
5. Turn chicken and baste with barbecue sauce.
6. Cover the chicken again and allow to cook for another 20 minutes.
7. Baste, cover and cook again for 30 minutes; repeat basting and turning during this time.
8. The chicken is done when the internal temperature of the chicken pieces are 165°F and juices run clear.
9. Baste with more barbecue sauce to serve!

Nutritional Info: Calories: 539, Sodium: 684mg, Dietary Fiber: 0.3g, Fat: 11.6g, Carbs: 15.1g, Protein: 87.6g.

CALIFORNIA SEARED CHICKEN

SERVINGS: 4

Prep time: 35 minutes
Cook time: 20 minutes

INGREDIENTS

4 boneless, skinless chicken breasts

3/4 cup balsamic vinegar

2 tablespoons extra virgin olive oil

1 tablespoon honey

1 teaspoon oregano

1 teaspoon basil

1 teaspoon garlic powder

FOR GARNISH:

Sea salt

Black pepper, fresh ground

4 slices fresh mozzarella cheese

4 slices avocado

4 slices beefsteak tomato

Balsamic glaze, for drizzling

Classic, ripe, and fresh California ingredients transform ordinary chicken into one scrumptious meal.

DIRECTIONS

1. Whisk together balsamic vinegar, honey, olive oil, oregano, basil and garlic powder in a large mixing bowl.
2. Add chicken to coat and marinate for 30 minutes in the refrigerator.
3. Preheat griddle to medium-high. Sear chicken for 7 minutes per side, or until a meat thermometer reaches 165°F.
4. Top each chicken breast with mozzarella, avocado, and tomato and tent with foil on the griddle to melt for 2 minutes.
5. Garnish with a drizzle of balsamic glaze, and a pinch of sea salt and black pepper.

Nutritional Info: Calories: 883, Sodium: 449mg, Dietary Fiber: 15.2g, Fat: 62.1g, Carbs: 29.8g, Protein: 55.3g.

SWEET CHILI LIME CHICKEN

SERVINGS: 4

Prep time: 35 minutes
Cook time: 15 minutes

INGREDIENTS

1/2 cup sweet chili sauce

1/4 cup soy sauce

1 teaspoon mirin

1 teaspoon orange juice, fresh squeezed

1 teaspoon orange marmalade

2 tablespoons lime juice

1 tablespoon brown sugar

1 clove garlic, minced

4 boneless, skinless chicken breasts

Sesame seeds, for garnish

Sweet and citrus marinated chicken is the perfect way to get some good use out of your outdoor griddle. Pair this citrus sweet medley with seared vegetables and brown rice for a quick weeknight meal.

DIRECTIONS

1. Whisk sweet chili sauce, soy sauce, mirin, orange marmalade, lime and orange juice, brown sugar, and minced garlic together in a small mixing bowl.
2. Set aside 1/4 cup of the sauce.
3. Toss chicken in sauce to coat and marinate 30 minutes.
4. Preheat your griddle to medium heat.
5. Put the chicken on the griddle and cook each side for 7 minutes.
6. Baste the cooked chicken with remaining marinade and garnish with sesame seeds to serve with your favorite sides.

Nutritional Info: Calories: 380, Sodium: 1274mg, Dietary Fiber: 0.5g, Fat: 12g, Carbs: 19.7g, Protein: 43.8g.

SEARED SPICY CITRUS CHICKEN

SERVINGS: 4

Prep time: 8 - 24 hours
Cook time: 20 minutes

Whip up something super-quick and easy for family dinner night. This is one delicious chicken recipe the whole family will love. Serve this delicious chicken with a side of grilled romaine or your favorite vegetables.

INGREDIENTS

2 lbs. boneless, skinless chicken thighs

FOR THE MARINADE:

1/4 cup fresh lime juice

2 teaspoon lime zest

1/4 cup honey

2 tablespoons olive oil

1 tablespoon balsamic vinegar

1/2 teaspoon sea salt

1/2 teaspoon black pepper

2 garlic cloves, minced

1/4 teaspoon onion powder

DIRECTIONS

1. Whisk together marinade ingredients in a large mixing bowl; reserve 2 tablespoons of the marinade for basting.
2. Add chicken and marinade to a sealable plastic bag and marinate 8 hours or overnight in the refrigerator.
3. Preheat griddle to medium high heat and brush lightly with olive oil.
4. Place chicken on griddle and cook 8 minutes per side.
5. Baste each side of chicken with reserved marinade during the last few minutes of cooking; chicken is done when the internal temperature reaches 165°F.
6. Plate chicken, tent with foil, and allow to rest for 5 minutes.
7. Serve and enjoy!

Nutritional Info: Calories: 381, Sodium: 337mg, Dietary Fiber: 1.1g, Fat: 20.2g, Carbs: 4.7g, Protein: 44.7g.

HONEY BALSAMIC MARINATED CHICKEN

SERVINGS: 4

Prep time: 30 minutes - 4 hours
Cook time: 20 minutes

Sweet honey meets balsamic vinegar for a delicious marinated chicken that is perfect for your outdoor griddle. Perfect served with your favorite sides or on a fluffy bed of brown rice.

INGREDIENTS

- 2 lbs. boneless, skinless chicken thighs
- 1 teaspoon olive oil
- 1/2 teaspoon sea salt
- 1/4 teaspoon black pepper
- 1/2 teaspoon paprika
- 3/4 teaspoon onion powder

FOR THE MARINADE:

- 2 tablespoons honey
- 2 tablespoons balsamic vinegar
- 2 tablespoons tomato paste
- 1 teaspoon garlic, minced

DIRECTIONS

1. Add chicken, olive oil, salt, black pepper, paprika, and onion powder to a sealable plastic bag. Seal and toss to coat, covering chicken with spices and oil; set aside.
2. Whisk together balsamic vinegar, tomato paste, garlic, and honey.
3. Divide the marinade in half. Add one half to the bag of chicken and store the other half in a sealed container in the refrigerator.
4. Seal the bag and toss chicken to coat. Refrigerate for 30 minutes to 4 hours.
5. Preheat a griddle to medium-high.
6. Discard bag and marinade. Add chicken to the griddle and cook 7 minutes per side or until juices run clear and a meat thermometer reads 165°F.
7. During last minute of cooking, brush remaining marinade on top of the chicken thighs.
8. Serve immediately.

Nutritional Info: Calories: 485, Sodium: 438mg, Dietary Fiber: 0.5g, Fat: 18.1g, Carbs: 11g, Protein: 66.1g.

SALSA VERDE MARINATED CHICKEN

SERVINGS: 6

Prep time: 4 hours 35 minutes
Cook time: 4 hours 50 minutes

INGREDIENTS

6 boneless, skinless chicken breasts

1 tablespoon olive oil

1 teaspoon sea salt

1 teaspoon chili powder

1 teaspoon ground cumin

1 teaspoon garlic powder

FOR THE SALSA VERDE MARINADE:

3 teaspoons garlic, minced

1 small onion, chopped

6 tomatillos, husked, rinsed and chopped

1 medium jalapeño pepper, cut in half, seeded

1/4 cup fresh cilantro, chopped

1/2 teaspoon sugar or sugar substitute

Spicy salsa Verde is the perfect complement to savory seared chicken. When you want to spice things up on the grill, this is just the recipe to help you add some spice to your life!

DIRECTIONS

1. Add Salsa Verde marinade ingredients to a food processor and pulse until smooth.
2. Mix sea salt, chili powder, cumin, and garlic powder together in a small mixing bowl. Season chicken breasts with olive oil and seasoning mix, and lay in glass baking dish.
3. Spread a tablespoon of Salsa Verde marinade over each chicken breast to cover; reserve remaining salsa for serving.
4. Cover dish with plastic wrap and refrigerate for 4 hours.
5. Preheat griddle to medium-high and brush with olive oil.
6. Add chicken to griddle and cook 7 minutes per side or until juices run clear and a meat thermometer reads 165°F.
7. Serve each with additional Salsa Verde and enjoy!

Nutritional Info: Calories: 321, Sodium: 444mg, Dietary Fiber: 1.3g, Fat: 13.7g, Carbs: 4.8g, Protein: 43g.

HASSELBACK STUFFED CHICKEN

SERVINGS: 4

Prep time: 15 minutes
Cook time: 30 minutes

INGREDIENTS

4 boneless, skinless chicken breasts

2 tablespoons olive oil

2 tablespoons taco seasoning

1/2 red, yellow and green pepper, very thinly sliced

1 small red onion, very thinly sliced

1/2 cup Mexican shredded cheese

Guacamole, for serving

Sour cream, for serving

Salsa, for serving

Who doesn't love chicken breast seasoned to perfection and grilled like hasselback potatoes? This delicious recipe is gluten-free and diabetic friendly for one delicious dinner that you can serve with salad or steamed veggies.

DIRECTIONS

1. Preheat griddle to med-high.
2. Cut thin horizontal cuts across each chicken breast; like you would hasselback potatoes.
3. Rub chicken evenly with olive oil and taco seasoning.
4. Add a mixture of bell peppers and red onions to each cut, and place the breasts on the griddle.
5. Cook chicken for 15 minutes.
6. Remove and top with cheese.
7. Tent loosely with foil and cook another 5 minutes, until cheese is melted.
8. Remove from griddle and top with guacamole, sour cream and salsa. Serve alongside your favorite side dishes!

Nutritional Info: Calories: 643, Sodium: 1549mg, Dietary Fiber: 3.8g, Fat: 18.6g, Carbs: 26.3g, Protein: 93.3g.

CREOLE CHICKEN STUFFED WITH CHEESE & PEPPERS

SERVINGS: 4

Prep time: 10 minutes
Cook time: 20 minutes

INGREDIENTS

4 boneless, skinless chicken breasts

8 mini sweet peppers, sliced thin and seeded

2 slices pepper jack cheese, cut in half

2 slices Colby jack cheese, cut in half

1 tablespoon creole seasoning, like Emeril's

1 teaspoon black pepper

1 teaspoon garlic powder

1 teaspoon onion powder

4 teaspoons olive oil, separated

Toothpicks

Nothing beats a stuffed chicken breast that preps in 10 minutes. This easy to assemble recipe will have your family eating healthy even on busy weeknights!

DIRECTIONS

1. Rinse chicken and pat dry.
2. Mix creole seasoning, pepper, garlic powder, and onion powder together in a small mixing bowl and set aside.
3. Cut a slit on the side of each chicken breast; be careful not to cut all the way through the chicken.
4. Rub each breast with 1 teaspoon each of olive oil.
5. Rub each chicken breast with seasoning mix and coat evenly.
6. Stuff each breast of chicken with 1 half pepper jack cheese slice, 1 half Colby cheese slice, and a handful of pepper slices.
7. Secure chicken shut with 4 or 5 toothpicks.
8. Preheat the griddle to medium-high and cook chicken for 8 minutes per side; or until chicken reaches an internal temperature of 165°F.
9. Allow chicken to rest for 5 minutes, remove toothpicks, and serve.

Nutritional Info: Calories: 509, Sodium:1117mg, Dietary Fiber: 3.4g, Fat: 25.1g, Carbs: 19.8g, Protein: 51.4g.

ROOT BEER CAN CHICKEN

SERVINGS: 2 - 4

Prep time: 8 hours and 10 minutes
Cook time: 20 minutes

INGREDIENTS

1 lb. boneless chicken thighs
3 (12 ounce) cans root beer, like A&W
Olive oil

FOR THE RUB:

1 tablespoon garlic powder
3/4 tablespoon sea salt
1/2 tablespoon white pepper
2 teaspoons smoked paprika
2 teaspoons garlic powder
1 teaspoon dried thyme
1/8 teaspoon cayenne pepper

A take on the traditional grilled root beer can chicken, this dish is just as delicious as the whole roasted version and packed with savory sweet flavor. Believe it or not, you can enjoy this scrumptious dish with mashed potatoes, a warm beet salad, roasted Brussel sprouts, and a delicious Malbec or Shiraz for one very romantic meal.

DIRECTIONS

1. Combine rub ingredients in a bowl; reserve half in a separate air tight container until ready to cook.
2. Rub chicken thighs evenly with olive oil and coat each with some rub.
3. Lay chicken in a 13 by 9 inch baking dish. Cover with 2 cans of root beer.
4. Preheat grill to medium-high heat.
5. Discard marinade and brush grill with olive oil.
6. Gently fold remaining rub and a half of the third can of root beer in a small bowl.
7. Sear chicken for 7 minutes on each side, basting often with root beer rub mix.
8. Serve when cooked through or chicken reaches 165°F and juices run clear

Nutritional Info: Calories: 363, Sodium: 1185mg, Dietary Fiber: 0.9g, Fat: 12.1g, Carbs: 29.9g, Protein: 33.4g.

CHIPOTLE ADOBE CHICKEN

SERVINGS: 4 - 6

Prep Time: 1 - 24 hours
Cook Time: 20 minutes

INGREDIENTS

2 lbs chicken thighs or breasts (boneless, skinless)

FOR THE MARINADE:

1/4 cup olive oil

2 chipotle peppers, in adobo sauce, plus 1 teaspoon adobo sauce from the can

1 tablespoon garlic, minced

1 shallot, finely chopped

1-1/2 tablespoons cumin

1 tablespoon cilantro, super-finely chopped or dried

2 teaspoons chili powder

1 teaspoon dried oregano

1/2 teaspoon salt

Fresh limes, garnish

Cilantro, garnish

Smoky sweet chipotle peppers in adobo sauce make for one delicious marinade! Perfect served with yellow Mexican rice or cheese enchiladas for one hearty Mexican inspired meal.

DIRECTIONS

1. Preheat griddle to medium-high.
2. Add marinade ingredients to a food processor or blender and pulse into a paste.
3. Add the chicken and marinade to a sealable plastic bag and massage to coat well.
4. Place in the refrigerator for 1 hour to 24 hours before cooking.
5. Sear chicken for 7 minutes, turn and cook and additional 7 minutes.
6. Turn heat to low and continue to cook until chicken has reached an internal temperature of 165°F.
7. Remove chicken from griddle and allow to rest 5 to 10 minutes before serving.
8. Garnish with a squeeze of fresh lime and a sprinkle of cilantro to serve.

Nutritional Info: Calories: 561, Sodium: 431mg, Dietary Fiber: 0.3g, Fat: 23.8g, Carbs: 18.7g, Protein: 65.9g.

SIZZLING CHICKEN FAJITAS

SERVINGS: 4

Prep time: 5 minutes
Cook time: 25 minutes

INGREDIENTS

4 boneless chicken breast halves, thinly sliced

1 yellow onion, sliced

1 large green bell pepper, sliced

1 large red bell pepper, sliced

1 teaspoon ground cumin

1 teaspoon garlic powder

1 teaspoon onion powder

2 tablespoons lime juice

1 tablespoon olive oil

1/2 teaspoon black pepper

1 teaspoon salt

3 tablespoons vegetable oil

10 flour tortillas

These chicken fajitas are sure to please everyone, and thanks to your outdoor griddle, you can make a single batch that's large enough for the whole family!

DIRECTIONS

1. In a zipper lock bag, combine the chicken, cumin, garlic, onion, lime juice, salt, pepper, and olive oil. Allow to marinate for 30 minutes.
2. Preheat griddle to medium heat.
3. On one side of the griddle add the olive oil and heat until shimmering. Add the onion and pepper and cook until slightly softened.
4. On the other side of the griddle add the marinated chicken and cook until lightly browned.
5. Once chicken is lightly browned, toss together with the onion and pepper and cook until chicken registers 165°F.
6. Remove chicken and vegetables from the griddle and serve with warm tortillas.

Nutritional Info: Calories: 408, Sodium: 664mg, Dietary Fiber: 5.5g, Fat: 18.3g, Carbs: 37.1g, Protein: 25.9g.

CHICKEN TACOS WITH AVOCADO CREMA

SERVINGS: 4 - 5

Prep Time: 1 hour 5 minutes
Cook Time: 10 minutes

INGREDIENTS

1 1/2 lbs. Boneless, skinless chicken breasts, sliced thin

FOR THE CHICKEN MARINADE:

1 serrano pepper, minced

2 teaspoons garlic, minced

1 lime, juiced

1 teaspoon ground cumin

1/3 cup olive oil

Sea salt, to taste

Black pepper, to taste

FOR THE AVOCADO CREMA:

1 cup sour cream

2 teaspoons lime juice

1 teaspoon lime zest

1 serrano pepper, diced and seeded

1 clove garlic, minced

1 large hass avocado

FOR THE GARNISH:

1/2 cup queso fresco, crumbled

2 teaspoons cilantro, chopped

1 lime sliced into wedges

10 corn tortillas

The perfect way to do lunch prep on a Sunday, you can whip this recipe up in no time and eat it for lunch all week. The whole family will enjoy these delicious tacos! Just keep your avocado crema in a sealable container until ready to assemble and you have easy healthy meals all week long.

DIRECTIONS

1. Mix chicken marinade together in a sealable plastic bag. Add chicken and toss to coat well.
2. Marinate for 1 hour in the refrigerator.
3. Combine avocado crema ingredients in a food processor or blender and pulse until smooth.
4. Cover and refrigerate until you are ready to assemble tacos.
5. Preheat griddle to medium heat and grill chicken for 5 minutes per side; rotating and turning as needed.
6. Remove from griddle and tent loosely with aluminum foil. Allow chicken to rest 5 minutes.
7. Serve with warm tortillas, a dollop of avocado crema, queso fresco, cilantro and lime wedges.
8. To meal prep: simply divide chicken into individual portion containers with a serving of the garnish, and take with tortillas wrapped in parchment paper to warm in a microwave to serve.

Nutritional Info: Calories: 703, Sodium: 357mg, Dietary Fiber: 6.3g, Fat: 44.5g, Carbs: 30.5g, Protein: 47.9g.

HAWAIIAN CHICKEN SKEWERS

SERVINGS: 4 - 5

Prep Time: 1 hour 10 minutes
Cook Time: 15 minutes

Cook up a taste of Hawaii with these delicious chicken skewers! Super-easy to make, you can enjoy these yummy skewers any night of the week - just prep them a day before cooking for one easy dinner in no time.

INGREDIENTS

1 lb. boneless, skinless chicken breast, cut into 1-1/2 inch cubes

3 cups pineapple, cut into 1-1/2 inch cubes

2 large green peppers, cut into 1-1/2 inch pieces

1 large red onion, cut into 1-1/2 inch pieces

2 tablespoons olive oil, to coat veggies

FOR THE MARINADE:

1/3 cup tomato paste

1/3 cup brown sugar, packed

1/3 cup soy sauce

1/4 cup pineapple juice

2 tablespoons olive oil

1-1/2 tablespoon mirin or rice wine vinegar

4 teaspoons garlic cloves, minced

1 tablespoon ginger, minced

1/2 teaspoon sesame oil

Pinch of sea salt

Pinch of ground black pepper

10 wooden skewers, for assembly

DIRECTIONS

1. Combine marinade ingredients in a mixing bowl until smooth. Reserve a 1/2 cup of the marinade in the refrigerator.
2. Add chicken and remaining marinade to a sealable plastic bag and refrigerate for 1 hour.
3. Soak 10 wooden skewer sticks in water for 1 hour.
4. Preheat the griddle to medium heat.
5. Add red onion, bell pepper and pineapple to a mixing bowl with 2 tablespoons olive oil and toss to coat.
6. Thread red onion, bell pepper, pineapple and chicken onto the skewers until all of the chicken has been used.
7. Place skewers on griddle and grab your reserved marinade from the refrigerator; cook for 5 minutes then brush with remaining marinade and rotate.
8. Brush again with marinade and sear about 5 additional minutes or until chicken reads 165°F on a meat thermometer.
9. Serve warm.

Nutritional Info: Calories: 311, Sodium: 1116mg, Dietary Fiber: 4.2g, Fat: 8.8g, Carbs: 38.1g, Protein: 22.8g.

FIERY ITALIAN CHICKEN SKEWERS

SERVINGS: 2 - 4

Prep time: 1 hour 20 minutes
Cook time: 20 minutes

INGREDIENTS

10 boneless, skinless chicken thighs, cut into chunks

1 large red onion, cut into wedges

1 large red pepper, stemmed, seeded, and cut into chunks

FOR THE MARINADE:

1/3 cup toasted pine nuts

1-1/2 cups sliced roasted red peppers

5 hot cherry peppers, stemmed and seeded, or to taste

1 cup packed fresh basil leaves, plus more to serve

4 cloves garlic, peeled

1/4 cup grated Parmesan cheese

1 tablespoon paprika

Extra virgin olive oil, as needed

Fire up some yummy chicken skewers on your outdoor griddle and really shake things up for lunch or dinner. You'll love how easy it is to make these perfectly seasoned skewers any day of the week.

DIRECTIONS

1. Combine the toasted pine nuts, roasted red peppers, hot cherry peppers, basil, garlic, Parmesan, and paprika in a food processor or blender and process until well-combined.

2. Add in olive oil until the pesto reaches a thin consistency in order to coat the chicken as a marinade.

3. Transfer half of the pesto to a large sealable plastic bag, and reserve the other half for serving.

4. Add the chicken thigh chunks to the bag of pesto, seal, and massage the bag to coat the chicken.

5. Refrigerate for 1 hour.

6. Preheat griddle to medium-high heat and brush with olive oil.

7. Thread the chicken cubes, red onion, and red pepper onto metal skewers.

8. Brush the chicken with the reserved pesto.

9. Cook until the chicken reaches an internal temperature of 165°F; about 5 minutes per side. Serve warm with your favorite salad or vegetables!

Nutritional Info: Calories: 945, Sodium: 798mg, Dietary Fiber: 3.2g, Fat: 46.7g, Carbs: 14.7g, Protein: 112.2g.

CHICKEN THIGHS WITH GINGER-SESAME GLAZE

SERVINGS: 4 - 8

Prep time: 10 minutes
Cook time: 20 minutes

INGREDIENTS

8 boneless, skinless chicken thighs

FOR THE GLAZE:

3 tablespoons dark brown sugar
2-1/2 tablespoons soy sauce
1 tablespoon fresh garlic, minced
2 teaspoons sesame seeds
1 teaspoon fresh ginger, minced
1 teaspoon Sambal Oelek
1/3 cup scallions, thinly sliced
Non-stick cooking spray

Ginger and sesame come together in this delicious glaze for a taste explosion. Serve this warm and sweet chicken with brown rice and your favorite vegetables for a quick, Asian-inspired meal.

DIRECTIONS

1. Combine glaze ingredients in a large mixing bowl; separate and reserve half for serving.
2. Add chicken to bowl and toss to coat well.
3. Preheat the griddle to medium-high heat.
4. Coat with cooking spray.
5. Cook chicken for 6 minutes on each side or until done.
6. Transfer chicken to plates and drizzle with remaining glaze to serve.

Nutritional Info: Calories: 301, Sodium: 413mg, Dietary Fiber: 0.3g, Fat: 11.2g, Carbs: 4.7g, Protein: 42.9g.

HONEY SRIRACHA GRILLED CHICKEN THIGHS

SERVINGS: 6

Prep: 5 minutes
Cook time: 35 minutes

INGREDIENTS

2.5 lbs. boneless chicken thighs
3 tablespoons butter, unsalted
1 tablespoon fresh ginger, minced
2 garlic cloves, minced
1/4 teaspoon smoked paprika
1/4 teaspoon chili powder
4 tablespoons honey
3 tablespoons Sriracha
1 tablespoon lime juice

Spicy sweet chicken thighs are not only super-tasty, but super-easy to whip up even when you are pressed for time. Simply marinate overnight and throw them on the griddle after work for a quick and easy restaurant quality meal right at home.

DIRECTIONS

1. Preheat griddle to medium high.
2. Melt butter in a small saucepan on medium low heat; when melted add ginger and garlic. Stir until fragrant, about 2 minutes.
3. Fold in smoked paprika, ground cloves, honey, Sriracha and lime juice. Stir to combine, turn heat to medium and simmer for 5 minutes.
4. Rinse and pat chicken thighs dry.
5. Season with salt and pepper on both sides.
6. Spray griddle with non-stick cooking spray.
7. Place chicken thighs on grill, skin side down first. Grill for 5 minutes. Flip the chicken over and grill on the other side for 5 minutes.
8. Continue to cook chicken, flipping every 3 minutes, so it doesn't burn, until the internal temperature reads 165°F on a meat thermometer.
9. During the last 5 minutes of grilling brush the glaze on both sides of the chicken.
10. Remove from grill and serve warm.

Nutritional Info: Calories: 375, Sodium: 221mg, Dietary Fiber: 0.3g, Fat: 22.5g, Carbs: 14.7g, Protein: 32g.

CHICKEN WINGS WITH SWEET RED CHILI AND PEACH GLAZE

SERVINGS: 4

Prep time: 15 minutes
Cook time: 30 minutes

INGREDIENTS

1 (12 oz.) jar peach preserves
1 cup sweet red chili sauce
1 teaspoon lime juice
1 tablespoon fresh cilantro, minced
1 (2-1/2 lb.) bag chicken wing sections
Non-stick cooking spray

Whip up delicious, restaurant style chicken wings right at home with your outdoor griddle. Sweet and savory, these chicken wings are the perfect treat for any game day or Sunday Funday with the family.

DIRECTIONS

1. Mix preserves, red chili sauce, lime juice and cilantro in mixing bowl. Divide in half, and place one half aside for serving.
2. Preheat griddle to medium heat and spray with non-stick cooking spray.
3. Cook wings for 25 minutes turning several times until juices run clear.
4. Remove wings from griddle, toss in a bowl to coat wings with remaining glaze.
5. Return wings to griddle and cook for an additional 3 to 5 minutes turning once.
6. Serve warm with your favorite dips and side dishes!

Nutritional Info: Calories: 790, Sodium: 643mg, Dietary Fiber: 1g, Fat: 16.9g, Carbs: 87.5g, Protein: 66g.

YELLOW CURRY CHICKEN WINGS

SERVINGS: 6

Prep time: 35 minutes
Cook time: 30 minutes to 1 hour

Warm and savory, these seared chicken wings are sure to spice things up with a taste of India. Curry Grilled Chicken Wings are best served with poppadoms, chutney, and raita dip for a delicious party snack.

INGREDIENTS

2 lbs. chicken wings

FOR THE MARINADE:

1/2 cup Greek yogurt, plain

1 tablespoon mild yellow curry powder

1 tablespoon olive oil

1/2 teaspoon sea salt

1/2 teaspoon black pepper

1 teaspoon red chili flakes

DIRECTIONS

1. Rinse and pat wings dry with paper towels.
2. Whisk marinade ingredients together in a large mixing bowl until well-combined.
3. Add wings to bowl and toss to coat.
4. Cover bowl with plastic wrap and chill in the refrigerator for 30 minutes.
5. Prepare one side of the griddle for medium heat and the other side on medium-high.
6. Working in batches, grill wings over medium heat, turning occasionally, until skin starts to brown; about 12 minutes.
7. Move wings to medium-high area of griddle for 5 minutes on each side to char until cooked through; meat thermometer should register 165°F when touching the bone.
8. Transfer wings to a platter and serve warm.

Nutritional Info: Calories: 324, Sodium: 292mg, Dietary Fiber: 0.4g, Fat: 14g, Carbs: 1.4g, Protein: 45.6g.

KOREAN GRILLED CHICKEN WINGS WITH SCALLION

SERVINGS: 6

Prep time: 30 minutes
Cook time: 30 minutes to 1 hour

INGREDIENTS

2 pounds chicken wings (flats and drumettes attached or separated)

FOR THE MARINADE:

1 tablespoon olive oil

1 teaspoon sea salt, plus more

1/2 teaspoon black pepper

1/2 cup gochujang, Korean hot pepper paste

1 scallion, thinly sliced, for garnish

Chicken wings are perfect when seasoned with the spice of Gochujang. This recipe pairs perfect with a Japanese White Sauce or cool, creamy sour cream infused with lime zest. Serve them up for your next tailgate or dinner party for something elevated and fun.

DIRECTIONS

1. Rinse and pat wings dry with paper towels.
2. Whisk marinade ingredients together in a large mixing bowl until well-combined.
3. Add wings to bowl and toss to coat.
4. Cover bowl with plastic wrap and chill in the refrigerator for 30 minutes.
5. Prepare one side of the griddle for medium heat and the other side on medium-high.
6. Working in batches, cook wings over medium heat, turning occasionally, until skin starts to brown; about 12 minutes.
7. Move wings to medium-high area of griddle for 5 minutes on each side to sear until cooked through; meat thermometer should register 165°F when touching the bone.
8. Transfer wings to a platter, garnish with scallions, and serve warm with your favorite dipping sauces.

Nutritional Info: Calories: 312, Sodium: 476mg, Dietary Fiber: 0.4g, Fat: 13.5g, Carbs: 1.1g, Protein: 43.9g.

KALE CAESAR SALAD WITH SEARED CHICKEN

SERVINGS: 1

Prep time: 10 minutes
Cook time: 8 minutes

INGREDIENTS

1 chicken breast
1 teaspoon garlic powder
1/2 teaspoon black pepper
1/2 teaspoon sea salt
2 kale leaves, chopped
shaved parmesan, for serving

FOR THE DRESSING:

1 tablespoon mayonnaise
1/2 tablespoon Dijon mustard
1/2 teaspoon garlic powder
1/2 teaspoon Worcestershire sauce
1/4 lemon, juice of (or 1/2 a small lime)
1/4 teaspoon anchovy paste
Pinch of sea salt
Pinch of black pepper

Light and airy, Caesar Salad is delicious tossed with seasoned, seared chicken and kale. You'll love this easy recipe that cooks up in no time - so you can enjoy healthy meals every day of the week!

DIRECTIONS

1. Mix garlic powder, black pepper, and sea salt in a small mixing bowl. Coat chicken with seasoning mix.
2. Preheat griddle to medium-high heat.
3. Sear chicken on each side for 7 minutes or until a meat thermometer reads 165°F when inserted in the thickest part of the breast.
4. Whisk all of the dressing ingredients together.
5. Plate your kale and pour the dressing over, and toss to combine.
6. Cut the chicken on a diagonal and place on top of the salad. Garnish with shaved parmesan, and serve.

Nutritional Info: Calories: 643, Sodium: 1549mg, Dietary Fiber: 3.8g, Fat: 18.6g, Carbs: 26.3g, Protein: 93.3g.

BUFFALO CHICKEN WINGS

SERVINGS: 6 - 8

Prep time: 10 minutes
Cook time: 20 minutes

INGREDIENTS

- 1 tablespoon sea salt
- 1 teaspoon ground black pepper
- 1 teaspoon garlic powder
- 3 lbs. chicken wings
- 6 tablespoons unsalted butter
- 1/3 cup buffalo sauce, like Moore's
- 1 tablespoon apple cider vinegar
- 1 tablespoon honey

Craving restaurant style Buffalo Wings?! You can easily whip them up right at home with this quick and easy recipe. Serve them with your favorite dips, carrots and celery for a fun treat.

DIRECTIONS

1. Combine salt, pepper and garlic powder in a large mixing bowl.
2. Toss the wings with the seasoning mixture to coat.
3. Preheat griddle to medium heat.
4. Place the wings on the griddle; make sure they are touching so the meat stays moist on the bone while grilling.
5. Flip wings every 5 minutes, for a total of 20 minutes of cooking.
6. Heat the butter, buffalo sauce, vinegar and honey in a saucepan over low heat; whisk to combine well.
7. Add wings to a large mixing bowl, toss the wings with the sauce to coat.
8. Turn griddle up to medium high and place wings back on the griddle until the skins crisp; about 1 to 2 minutes per side.
9. Add wings back into the bowl with the sauce and toss to serve.

Nutritional Info: Calories: 410, Sodium: 950mg, Dietary Fiber: 0.2g, Fat: 21.3g, Carbs: 2.7g, Protein: 49.4g.

SEARED CHICKEN WITH FRUIT SALSA

SERVINGS: 4

Prep time: 1 hour
Cook time: 20 minutes

Fruit salsa is the perfect complement to any chicken dish. This zesty recipe is sure to knock the socks off the ones you love for a delicious healthy weekend meal on the griddle! Simply serve with grilled veggies on the side for a healthy treat.

INGREDIENTS

4 boneless, skinless chicken breasts

FOR THE MARINADE:

1/2 cup fresh lemon juice

1/2 cup soy sauce

1 tablespoon fresh ginger, minced

1 tablespoon lemon pepper seasoning

2 garlic cloves, minced

FOR THE SALSA:

1-1/2 cups pineapple, chopped

3/4 cup kiwi fruit, chopped

1/2 cup mango, chopped

1/2 cup red onion, finely chopped

2 tablespoons fresh cilantro, chopped

1 small jalapeño pepper, seeded and chopped

1-1/2 teaspoons ground cumin

1/4 teaspoon sea salt

1/8 teaspoon black pepper

1/2 teaspoon olive oil, more for brushing griddle

DIRECTIONS

1. Combine marinade ingredients in a large sealable plastic bag.
2. Add chicken to bag, seal, and toss to coat. Marinate in refrigerator for 1 hour.
3. Combine salsa ingredients in a mixing bowl and toss gently to combine. Set aside until ready to serve.
4. Preheat the griddle to medium heat.
5. Remove chicken from bag and discard marinade.
6. Brush griddle with olive oil and cook chicken for 7 minutes on each side or until chicken is cooked through.
7. Serve chicken topped with salsa alongside your favorite side dishes.

Nutritional Info: Calories: 391, Sodium: 2051mg, Dietary Fiber: 3.7g, Fat: 12.3g, Carbs: 23.6g, Protein: 46.1g.

TERIYAKI CHICKEN AND VEGGIE RICE BOWLS

SERVINGS: 4

Prep time: 8 hours 10 minutes
Cook time: 20 minutes

INGREDIENTS

1 bag brown rice

FOR THE SKEWERS:

2 boneless skinless chicken breasts, cubed

1 red onion, quartered

1 red pepper, cut into cube slices

1 green pepper, cut into cube slices

1/2 pineapple, cut into cubes

FOR THE MARINADE:

1/4 cup light soy sauce

1/4 cup sesame oil

1 tablespoon ginger, fresh grated

1 garlic clove, crushed

1/2 lime, juiced

Rice bowls are both delicious and nutritious and a perfect way to meal prep on a Sunday for the whole week. This recipe will keep in your refrigerator for up to 4 days once cooked and makes for a delicious meal at work or school when microwaved!

DIRECTIONS

1. Whisk the marinade ingredients together in a small mixing bowl.
2. Add chicken and marinade to a resealable plastic bag, seal and toss well to coat.
3. Refrigerate for one hour or overnight.
4. Prepare rice as instructed on the bag.
5. Preheat the griddle to medium-high heat.
6. Thread the chicken and the cubed veggies onto 8 metal skewers and cook for 8 minutes on each side until seared and cooked through.
7. Portion rice out into bowls and top with two skewers each, and enjoy!

Nutritional Info: Calories: 477, Sodium: 362mg, Dietary Fiber: 3.8g, Fat: 20.6g, Carbs: 48.1g, Protein: 26.1g.

CHICKEN SATAY WITH ALMOND BUTTER SAUCE

SERVINGS: 4

Prep time: 2 hours 20 minutes
Cook time: 8 minutes

A mouthwatering, sweet meets spicy delight - this recipe is delicious served as an appetizer for dipping or over a bed of pad Thai noodles for an Asian-inspired dish. Serve it garnished with lime wedges and crushed peanuts for something out of this world.

INGREDIENTS

1 lb. boneless, skinless chicken thighs, cut into thin strips

Olive oil, for brushing

FOR THE MARINADE:

1/2 cup canned light coconut milk

1/2 lime, juiced

1 tablespoon honey

2 teaspoons soy sauce

1-1/2 teaspoons fish sauce

1/2 teaspoon red chili flakes

2 teaspoons ginger, grated

1 clove of garlic, grated

1/2 teaspoon curry powder

1/4 teaspoon ground coriander

FOR THE ALMOND BUTTER SAUCE:

1/4 cup almond butter

1/4 cup water

2 tablespoons canned, light coconut milk

1 tablespoon honey

1/2 lime, juiced

1 teaspoon fish sauce

1 teaspoon fresh grated ginger

1/2 teaspoon low sodium soy sauce

1/2 teaspoon Sriracha

DIRECTIONS

1. Whisk together all of the ingredients for the marinade in a medium mixing bowl.
2. Add chicken to mixing bowl and toss to coat.
3. Cover and refrigerate 2 hours or overnight.
4. Preheat griddle to medium high heat and brush with olive oil.
5. Thread the chicken strips onto metal skewers.
6. Place the chicken skewers on the prepared griddle and cook 3 minutes, rotate, and cook another 4 minutes or until the chicken is cooked through.
7. Whisk together all of the ingredients for the almond butter sauce in a small saucepan.
8. Bring the sauce to a boil on medium heat, then lower to medium low and simmer for 1 to 2 minutes or until the sauce thickens.
9. Serve chicken satay warm with the almond butter sauce and enjoy.

Nutritional Info: Calories: 347, Sodium: 743mg, Dietary Fiber: 1.2g, Fat: 19.7g, Carbs: 8.6g, Protein: 34.3g.

CHICKEN FRIED RICE

SERVINGS: 4

Prep time: 10 minutes
Cook time: 20 minutes

INGREDIENTS

2 boneless, skinless chicken breasts, cut into small pieces

4 cups long grain rice, cooked and allowed to air dry

1/3 cup soy sauce

1 yellow onion, finely chopped

4 cloves garlic, finely chopped

1 cups petite peas

2 carrots sliced into thin rounds

1/2 cup corn kernels

1/4 cup vegetable oil

2 tablespoons butter

A large, wide griddle is the perfect way to make a big batch of fried rice for the whole family. Your outdoor griddle will ensure your rice is perfectly cooked and savory.

DIRECTIONS

1. Preheat griddle to medium-high.
2. Add the vegetable oil to the griddle.
3. When the oil is shimmering, add the onion, carrot, peas, and corn.
4. Cook for several minutes, until lightly charred.
5. Add the chicken and cook until just browned.
6. Add the rice, soy sauce, garlic, and butter.
7. Toss until the rice is tender and the vegetables are just softened.
8. Serve immediately.

Nutritional Info: Calories: 485, Sodium: 1527mg, Dietary Fiber: 4.7g, Fat: 20.8g, Carbs: 60.9g, Protein: 13.4g.

CHAPTER 7

MAIN DISHES: BEEF

BASIC JUICY NY STRIP STEAK

SERVINGS 1

Prep time: 45 minutes
Cook time: 8 minutes

INGREDIENTS

1 (8 ounce) NY strip steak
Olive oil
Sea salt
Fresh ground black pepper

When you are craving a basic, juicy steak with no frills - this is the recipe to try out on your outdoor griddle. Simple and succulent, this steak is for those who love bare bones seasoning without sacrificing flavor.

DIRECTIONS

1. Remove the steak from the refrigerator and let it come to room temperature, about 30 to 45 minutes.
2. Preheat griddle to medium-high heat and brush with olive oil.
3. Season the steak on all sides with salt and pepper.
4. Cook steak about 4 to 5 minutes.
5. Flip and cook about 4 minutes more for medium rare steak; between 125°F and 130°F on a meat thermometer.
6. Transfer the steak to a plate and let it rest for 5 minutes before serving.

Nutritional Info: Calories: 1560, Sodium: 8468mg, Dietary Fiber: 0g, Fat: 86g, Carbs: 0.1g, Protein: 184g.

HIGH-LOW STRIP STEAK

SERVINGS: 2

Prep time: 8 - 12 hours
Cook time: 15 minutes

INGREDIENTS

2 (1-pound) New York strip steaks, trimmed

FOR THE RUB:

1 bunch thyme sprigs

1 bunch rosemary sprigs

1 bunch sage sprigs

1 1/2 teaspoons black pepper, divided

3/4 teaspoon sea salt, divided

1/2 teaspoon garlic powder

2 tablespoons chopped fresh flat-leaf parsley

2 tablespoons extra-virgin olive oil

High-low strip steaks are the perfect way to quickly grill up a delicious NY Strip steak. Scrumptiously seasoned, these steaks pair deliciously with creamy mashed potatoes and grilled asparagus.

DIRECTIONS

1. Preheat griddle to high heat.
2. Combine rub ingredients in a small mixing bowl and rub steaks with spice mixture; let rest 10 minutes.
3. Place steaks on grill and cook 1 minute per side.
4. Turn griddle down to medium heat.
5. Turn steaks and grill 3 additional minutes per side; or until thermometer registers 135°F for medium rare.
6. Remove steaks to a platter.
7. Let rest 5 minutes. Cut steaks across grain into thin slices.

Nutritional Info: Calories: 347, Sodium: 831mg, Dietary Fiber: 1.9g, Fat: 20.4g, Carbs: 3.7g, Protein: 38.7g.

TUSCAN-STYLE STEAK WITH CRISPY POTATOES

SERVINGS: 4

Prep time: 30 minutes
Cook time: 35 minutes

INGREDIENTS

2 bone-in porterhouse steaks

1 1/2 lb. small potatoes, like Yukon Gold, scrubbed but skins left on, halved

4 tablespoons extra-virgin olive oil, divided

Sea salt and freshly ground pepper, to taste

2 teaspoons red wine, like Sangiovese or Montepulciano

1 teaspoon balsamic vinegar

Pinch red pepper flakes

3 fresh rosemary sprigs, needles removed (discard stems)

Sweet and savory, this recipe calls for an Italian twist on classic meat and potatoes you'll absolutely love.

DIRECTIONS

1. Add potatoes to a large pot and cover with water, bring to a boil over high heat, then reduce the heat to medium-high and cook until the potatoes are almost tender, about 10 minutes. Drain, add to a medium mixing bowl, coat with 2 tablespoons olive oil, and set aside.
2. Preheat griddle to medium heat.
3. Whisk 2 tablespoons olive oil, rosemary, red wine, vinegar, and pepper flakes; add steaks to marinade and set aside until ready to cook.
4. Sprinkle potatoes with salt and pepper.
5. Add steaks to one side of the griddle and potatoes to the other.
6. Cook steak for 5 minutes, flip and 4 minutes on the other side for medium rare.
7. Add the potatoes to cook for 5 minutes.
8. Transfer steaks to a cutting board and tent with aluminum foil and let rest for 5 minutes while potatoes are cooking.
9. Divide each steak into 2 pieces and divide among 4 dinner plates. Spoon some potatoes around the steak and serve hot!

Nutritional Info: Calories: 366, Sodium: 153mg, Dietary Fiber: 4.5g, Fat: 23.3g, Carbs: 27.3g, Protein: 13.4g.

CAPRESE GRILLED FILET MIGNON

SERVINGS: 4

Prep time: 10 minutes
Cook time: 10 minutes

INGREDIENTS

4 (6 ounce) filets

1 teaspoon garlic salt

Italian Olive oil

2 Roma tomatoes, sliced

4 ounces fresh buffalo mozzarella, cut into four slices

8 fresh basil leaves

Balsamic vinegar glaze, for drizzling

Sea salt, for seasoning

Fresh ground pepper

Serve up something healthy, with these tender fillets topped with a taste of the Mediterranean. Serve with creamy risotto, succulent grilled scallops and your favorite red wine for a surf and turf dream meal right at home.

DIRECTIONS

1. Lightly brush each filet, on all sides, with olive oil and rub with garlic salt.
2. Preheat griddle to high. Place steaks on griddle, reduce heat to medium, tent with foil and cook for 5 minutes.
3. Flip, re-tent, and cook for an additional 5 minutes; during the last 2 minutes of grilling top each with a slice of mozzarella.
4. Remove steaks from the griddle and top each with a few tomato slices, 2 basil leaves.
5. Drizzle with balsamic, sprinkle with sea salt and black pepper and serve.

Nutritional Info: Calories: 406, Sodium: 688mg, Dietary Fiber: 0.8g, Fat: 21.8g, Carbs: 7.2g, Protein: 45.1g.

RIB-EYE STEAK WITH HERBED STEAK BUTTER

SERVINGS: 2 - 4

Prep time: 12 hours
Cook time: 50 minutes

INGREDIENTS

1 (24-ounce) bone-in Tomahawk rib-eye, about 2-1/2 inches thick

Olive oil

Sea salt

Fresh cracked pepper

3 tablespoons premium French butter

1/2 teaspoon Herbes de Provence

Cooking rib-eye on a griddle is one of the best ways to achieve a tender and delicious steak - especially topped with creamy, herbed French butter. Serve with mashed potatoes and the grilled asparagus recipe below for one delicious meal.

DIRECTIONS

1. Beat butter with herbs in a small mixing bowl, cover and refrigerate until ready to grill rib-eye.
2. Rub the rib-eye liberally with olive oil, salt and pepper until entire steak is covered.
3. Wrap lightly with cling wrap and place in the refrigerator to marinate for 12 hours.
4. Preheat the griddle to high heat on one side and medium low on the other side, at least one hour prior to cooking.
5. Remove the steak from the refrigerator and leave at room temperature during the hour that the griddle is preheating.
6. Place the steak on the center of the hottest side of the griddle. Do this for both sides, about 10 minutes.
7. Move the rib-eye to the cooler side of the griddle and cook to rare, about 25 to 30 minutes.
8. Transfer rib-eye to a grill rack, add herbed butter on top, and lightly tent it with tin foil to rest for at least 15 minutes before carving.
9. Serve with your favorite sides!

Nutritional Info: Calories: 549, Sodium: 607mg, Dietary Fiber: 1.5g, Fat: 40.3g, Carbs: 3.5g, Protein: 40.9g.

TEPPANYAKI BEEF WITH VEGETABLES

SERVINGS: 6

Prep time: 10 minutes
Cook time: 15 minutes

INGREDIENTS

STEAK:

2 - 1 lb. sirloin steaks

1 tablespoon garlic powder

4 tablespoons soy sauce

1 white onion, sliced into large rounds

3 zucchinis, sliced into 1/4 inch thick flats

2 cups snap peas

4 tablespoons vegetable oil

3 tablespoons butter

Salt and black pepper

If you've ever been to a Teppan steak house, you know how much fun it can be. Luckily, your outdoor griddle allows you to have all of that Teppanyaki fun at home.

DIRECTIONS

1. Season the steak with salt, pepper, and garlic powder.
2. Set your griddle to high heat on one side and medium-high heat on the other side.
3. Add some vegetable oil to the medium-hot side and add the onion rings, zucchini, and snap peas. Season with a little salt and pepper.
4. Add the steaks to the hot side and cook for 3 minutes. Flip, top with butter and add soy sauce to the steaks. Continue cooking an additional 4 minutes.
5. Remove the steak and vegetables from the griddle and slice the steak across the grain before serving.

Nutritional Info: Calories: 484, Sodium: 755mg, Dietary Fiber: 4.2g, Fat: 24.7g, Carbs: 13.8g, Protein: 50.9g.

TENDER STEAK WITH PINEAPPLE RICE

SERVINGS: 4

Prep time: 10 minutes
Cook time: 10 minutes

INGREDIENTS

4 (4-ounce) beef fillets

1/4 cup soy sauce

1/2 teaspoon black pepper

1/2 teaspoon garlic powder

1 (8-ounce) can pineapple chunks, in juice, drained

2 scallions, thin sliced

2 (8.8-ounce) packages pre-cooked brown rice, like Uncle Ben's

7/8 teaspoon kosher salt

Olive oil, for brushing

Sticky, sweet pineapple rice is one delicious compliment to tender grilled steak. You'll definitely impress family and friends with this yummy recipe when you serve it with grilled veggies and iced green tea.

DIRECTIONS

1. Combine soy sauce, pepper, garlic powder, and beef in a large sealable plastic bag.
2. Seal and massage sauce into beef; let stand at room temperature for 7 minutes, turning bag occasionally.
3. Preheat griddle to medium-high heat and brush with olive oil.
4. Add pineapple and green onions to grill and cook 5 minutes or until well charred, turning to char evenly.
5. Remove pineapple mix and brush with additional olive oil.
6. Add steaks and cook 3 minutes on each side, for rare, or until desired temperature is reached.
7. Cook rice according to package instructions.
8. Add rice, pineapple, onions, and salt to a bowl and stir gently to combine.
9. Plate steaks with pineapple rice and serve!

Nutritional Info: Calories: 369, Sodium: 1408mg, Dietary Fiber: 2.1g, Fat: 12.4g, Carbs: 37g, Protein: 27.9g.

CAPRESE FLANK STEAK

SERVINGS: 4

Prep time: 10 minutes
Cook time: 10 minutes

INGREDIENTS

4 (6 ounce) flank steaks

Sea salt, for seasoning

Flakey sea salt, for serving

Fresh ground pepper

Olive oil

2 Roma tomatoes, sliced

4 ounces fresh buffalo mozzarella, cut into four slices

8 fresh basil leaves

Balsamic vinegar glaze, for drizzling

A super-fresh take on steak, this recipe elevates the delicious flank cut of steak to a whole new level. Best served with grilled eggplant, salad, pasta and a glass of Sangiovese for one decadent, Italian-inspired meal.

DIRECTIONS

1. Lightly brush each filet, on all sides, with olive oil and season with salt and pepper.
2. Preheat griddle to high. Place steaks on griddle, reduce heat to medium, tent with foil and cook for 5 minutes.
3. Flip, re-tent, and cook for an additional 5 minutes; during the last 2 minutes of cooking, top each with a slice of mozzarella.
4. Remove steaks from the griddle and top each with a few tomato slices, 2 basil leaves.
5. Drizzle with balsamic glaze, and sprinkle with flaky salt and a little more black pepper.

Nutritional Info: Calories: 461, Sodium: 485 mg, Dietary Fiber: 0.8g, Fat: 22.8g, Carbs: 5.7g, Protein: 55.9g.

FLANK STEAK WITH GARLIC AND ROSEMARY

SERVINGS: 4

Prep time: 10 minutes
Cook time: 20 minutes

INGREDIENTS

2 (8 ounce) flank steaks

FOR THE MARINADE:

1 tablespoon extra-virgin olive oil, plus more for brushing

2 tablespoons fresh rosemary, chopped

4 cloves garlic, minced

2 teaspoons sea salt

1/4 teaspoon black pepper

Flavorful and delicious, the flank steak is perfect complimented with robust garlic and spicy rosemary. Serve on top of a bed or your favorite greens dressed with balsamic vinegar and olive oil for one very healthy meal.

DIRECTIONS

1. Add marinade ingredients to a food processor or blender and pulse until garlic and rosemary are pulverized.
2. Use a fork to pierce the steaks 10 times on each side.
3. Rub each evenly with the marinade on both sides.
4. Place in a covered dish and refrigerate for at least 1 hour or overnight.
5. Preheat griddle to high and brush with olive oil and preheat to high.
6. Cook steaks for 5 minutes, flip, tent with foil, and cook for about 3-4 minutes more.
7. Transfer meat to rest on a cutting board, cover with aluminum foil, for about 15 minutes.
8. Slice very thin against the grain and serve immediately.

Nutritional Info: Calories: 260, Sodium: 1001mg, Dietary Fiber: 0.8g, Fat: 13.2g, Carbs: 2.1g, Protein: 31.8g.

GREEK FLANK STEAK GYROS

SERVINGS: 4

Prep Time: 5 minutes
Cook Time: 20 minutes

INGREDIENTS

1 pound flank steak

1 white onion, thinly sliced

1 Roma tomato, thinly sliced

1 cucumber, peeled and thinly sliced

1/4 cup crumbled feta cheese

4 6-inch pita pockets

FOR THE MARINADE:

1/4 cup olive oil, plus more for brushing

1 teaspoon dried oregano

1 teaspoon balsamic vinegar

1 teaspoon garlic powder

Sea salt and freshly ground pepper, to taste

FOR THE SAUCE:

1 cup plain yogurt

2 tablespoons fresh dill (can use dried), chopped

1 teaspoon garlic, minced

2 tablespoons lemon juice

Grilled flank steak makes for the perfect protein to stuff inside warmed pita pockets. When you're craving a taste of Greece be sure to serve this alongside hummus and carrots with a glass of sparkling water and lemon.

DIRECTIONS

1. Cut the flank steak into thin strips against the grain. Add the marinade ingredients to a large sealable plastic bag, add the sliced meat, seal, and turn to coat.
2. Place in the refrigerator to marinate for 2 hours or overnight.
3. Preheat the griddle to medium-high heat, and an oven to 250°F.
4. Combine the sauce ingredients in small mixing bowl and set aside.
5. Spritz the pitas with a little water, wrap in foil and place in the oven to warm.
6. Brush griddle with olive oil.
7. Add meat to grill and discard marinade. Cook until brown and cooked through, about 5 minutes.
8. Remove the pitas from the oven and cut in half.
9. Arrange the pitas on plates and stuff with cucumber, tomato, onions, and beef.
10. Spoon some yogurt sauce over the meat and top with feta and serve.

Nutritional Info: Calories: 901, Sodium: 1221mg, Dietary Fiber: 5.7g, Fat: 27.2g, Carbs: 107.8g, Protein: 53.5g.

TEXAS-STYLE BRISKET

SERVINGS: 6

Prep time: 10 minutes
Cook time: 6 hours 20 minutes

INGREDIENTS

1 (4-1/2 lb) flat cut beef brisket (about 3 inches thick)

FOR THE RUB:

1 tablespoon sea salt

1 tablespoon dark brown sugar

2 teaspoons smoked paprika

2 teaspoons chili powder

1 teaspoon garlic powder

1 teaspoon onion powder

1 teaspoon ground black pepper

1 teaspoon mesquite liquid smoke, like Colgin

Coffee makes for a decadent rub when it comes to seasoning juicy steak to perfection. Slow cooked on low heat all day, you'll love making this for your next backyard barbecue or family fun day at home.

DIRECTIONS

1. Combine the rub ingredients in a small mixing bowl.
2. Rinse and pat brisket dry and rub with coffee mix.
3. Preheat the griddle for two zone cooking; heat one side to high and leaving one side with low heat.
4. Sear on high heat side for 3 - 5 minutes on each side or until nicely charred.
5. Move to low heat side, tent with foil, and cook for 6 hours or until a meat thermometer registers 195°F.
6. Remove from griddle. Let stand, covered, 30 minutes.
7. Cut brisket across grain into thin slices and serve.

Nutritional Info: Calories: 591, Sodium: 3953mg, Dietary Fiber: 0.7g, Fat: 42.8g, Carbs: 3.2g, Protein: 45.9g.

FLASH-MARINATED SKIRT STEAK

SERVINGS: 4

Prep time: 30 minutes
Cook time: 45 minutes

INGREDIENTS

2 (8 ounce) skirt steaks

FOR THE MARINADE:

2 tablespoons balsamic vinegar

2 teaspoons olive oil, more for brushing

2 garlic cloves, minced

Sea salt, to taste

Black pepper, to taste

Flash marinated flank steak is the perfect steak when your pressed for time. Quick and easy to marinate, don't be afraid to prepare the recipe in the morning and cook it right after work!

DIRECTIONS

1. Combine marinade ingredients in a sealable plastic bag, add steaks, seal bag, turn to coat; let stand at room temperature for 30 minutes.
2. Preheat griddle to medium-high heat.
3. Remove steaks and discard marinade, place on griddle and cook about 3 minutes per side. Transfer steaks to cutting board and rest for 5 Minutes.
4. Cut across the grain into slices and serve with your favorite sides.

Nutritional Info: Calories: 256, Sodium: 204mg, Dietary Fiber: 0g, Fat: 13.8g, Carbs: 0.6g, Protein: 30.3g.

COFFEE CRUSTED SKIRT STEAK

SERVINGS: 8

Prep time: 10 minutes
Cook time: 20 minutes

INGREDIENTS

1/4 cup coffee beans, finely ground

1/4 cup dark brown sugar, firmly packed

1-1/2 teaspoon sea salt

1/8 teaspoon ground cinnamon

Pinch cayenne pepper

2-1/2 lb. skirt steak, cut into 4 pieces

1 tablespoon olive oil

Serve up something delicious for dinner when you grill up skirt steak crusted with rich ground coffee. You'll love this recipe served with a side of brown rice and a glass of Malbec or sparkling water.

DIRECTIONS

1. Heat griddle to high.
2. Combine coffee, brown sugar, salt, cinnamon, and cayenne pepper in a bowl to make rub.
3. Remove steak from refrigerator and let come to room temperature, about 15 minutes. Rub steak with oil, and sprinkle with spice rub. Massage spice rub into meat.
4. Sear until charred and medium-rare, 2 to 4 minutes per side. Transfer to a cutting board, cover with foil and let rest 5 minutes before thinly slicing against the grain.

Nutritional Info: Calories: 324, Sodium: 461mg, Dietary Fiber: 0.1g, Fat: 16g, Carbs: 4.6g, Protein: 37.9g.

CARNE ASADA

SERVINGS: 4

Prep time: 1 - 2 hours
Cook time: 15 minutes

INGREDIENTS

1 lb. hanger steak or shirt steak
1/4 cup olive oil
1 lime, juiced
1 orange, juiced
1 garlic clove, finely chopped
1/2 teaspoon cumin
1/4 teaspoon salt
1/4 teaspoon ground pepper
Handful of fresh cilantro, chopped

Grill up a taste of Mexico with this delicious Carne Asada recipe. Charred steak, seasoned to perfection can be served as a main dish or as the ingredient in several of your favorite Mexican inspired meals like tacos and burritos.

DIRECTIONS

1. Combine all of the ingredients in a large sealable plastic bag. Marinate in the refrigerator for 1 to 2 hours.
2. Preheat to medium/high heat, cook for 3 minutes on each side or until just cooked through.
3. Transfer to cutting board to rest for 10 minutes.
4. Slice against the grain and serve.

Nutritional Info: Calories: 363, Sodium: 200mg, Dietary Fiber: 1.7g, Fat: 18.4g, Carbs: 7.7g, Protein: 41.6g.

MEXICAN STEAK SALAD

SERVINGS: 2

Prep time: 10 minutes
Cook time: 10 minutes

INGREDIENTS

STEAK MARINADE:

2 tablespoons olive oil

3 garlic cloves, minced

2 teaspoons chili powder

1 teaspoon ground cumin

1 teaspoon kosher salt

1 teaspoon freshly ground pepper

1-1/2 pounds skirt or flap steak, cut into 4-inch lengths

1/2 cup lager beer

SALAD:

12 ounces romaine hearts, trimmed and chopped

1 can black beans, drained and rinsed

1 pint cherry tomatoes, halved

1 large ripe avocado, pitted, peeled, and cut into chunks

About 1/3 cup crumbled queso fresco

Chopped fresh cilantro, for garnish

Kosher salt

DRESSING:

1/2 cup plain whole milk yogurt

1/3 cup chopped fresh cilantro

Zest of 1 lime

Juice of 2 limes

Juicy steak is the perfect way to top a Mexican-inspired salad. Spice meets creamy avocado dressing for a healthy way to enjoy steak for both lunch and dinner!

DIRECTIONS

1. Make marinade, then marinate steak for 4 hours to overnight.
2. Combine salad ingredients in a large bowl; add dressing and mix well. Place salad on separate plates.
3. Preheat griddle to high. Place marinated steak on griddle, reduce heat to medium, tent with foil and cook for 5 minutes.
4. Flip, re-tent, and cook for an additional 5 minutes.
5. Remove steak from the griddle and slice into 2 inch strips.
6. Place steak strips on individual salads, and sprinkle with flakey salt and a little black pepper. Garnish with cilantro.

Nutritional Info: Calories: 1332, Sodium: 2011mg, Dietary Fiber: 13.3g, Fat: 65.1g, Carbs: 29.4g, Protein: 152.3g.

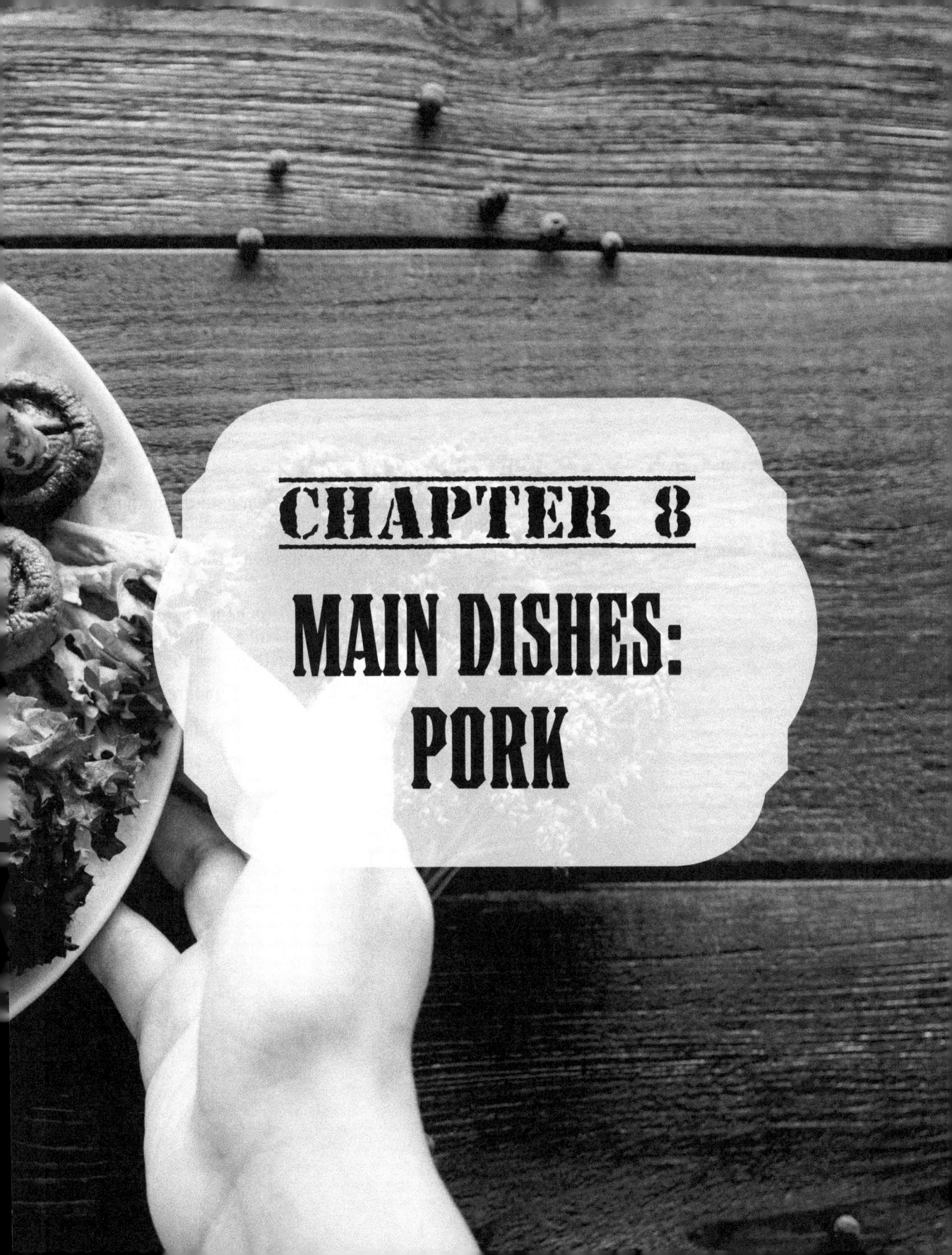

CHAPTER 8

MAIN DISHES: PORK

PORK TENDERLOIN SANDWICHES

SERVINGS: 6

Prep time: 10 minutes
Cook time: 25 minutes

INGREDIENTS

2 (3/4-lb.) pork tenderloins

1 teaspoon garlic powder

1 teaspoon sea salt

1 teaspoon dry mustard

1/2 teaspoon coarsely ground pepper

Olive oil, for brushing

6 whole wheat hamburger buns

6 tablespoons barbecue sauce

Tender grilled pork is the perfect way to grill up a savory sandwich on your outdoor griddle. This simple, yet flavorful sandwich will have you grilling like a gourmet chef in no time.

DIRECTIONS

1. Stir the garlic, salt, pepper, and mustard together in a small mixing bowl.
2. Rub pork tenderloins evenly with olive oil, then seasoning mix.
3. Preheat griddle to medium-high heat, and cook 10 to 12 minutes on each side or until a meat thermometer inserted into thickest portion registers 155°F.
4. Remove from grill and let stand 10 minutes.
5. Slice thinly, and evenly distribute onto hamburger buns.
6. Drizzle each sandwich with barbecue sauce and serve.

Nutritional Info: Calories: 372, Sodium: 694mg, Dietary Fiber: 2.9g, Fat: 13.4g, Carbs: 24.7g, Protein: 37.2g.

HERB-CRUSTED MEDITERRANEAN PORK TENDERLOIN

SERVINGS: 4

Prep time: 2 hours
Cook time: 30 minutes

INGREDIENTS

1 pound pork tenderloin
1 tablespoon olive oil
2 teaspoons dried oregano
3/4 teaspoon lemon pepper
1 teaspoon garlic powder
1/4 cup parmesan cheese, grated
3 tablespoons olive tapenade

Herb-Crusted Tenderloin with Mediterranean style spices is one great way to grill up juicy tenderloin. My favorite way to serve this dish is alongside lemon chili pasta and salad with a glass of Pinot Grigio.

DIRECTIONS

1. Place pork on a large piece of plastic wrap.
2. Rub tenderloin with oil, and sprinkle oregano, garlic powder, and lemon pepper evenly over entire tenderloin.
3. Wrap tightly in the plastic wrap and refrigerate for 2 hours.
4. Preheat griddle to medium-high heat.
5. Transfer pork to cutting board, remove plastic wrap, and make a lengthwise cut through center of tenderloin, opening meat so it lies flat, but do not cut all the way through.
6. Combine tapenade and parmesan in a small mixing bowl; rub into the center of the tenderloin and fold meat back together.
7. Tie together with twine in 2-inch intervals.
8. Sear tenderloin for 20 minutes, turning tenderloin once during grilling, or until internal temperature reaches 145°F.
9. Transfer tenderloin to cutting board.
10. Tent with foil; let rest for 10 minutes.
11. Remove string and cut into 1/4-inch-thick slices and serve.

Nutritional Info: Calories: 413, Sodium: 1279mg, Dietary Fiber: 0.5g, Fat: 30.5g, Carbs: 2.4g, Protein: 31.4g.

PAPRIKA DIJON PORK TENDERLOIN

SERVINGS: 6

Prep time: 10 minutes
Cook time: 4 hours

INGREDIENTS

2 1 lb pork tenderloins

2 tablespoons Dijon mustard

1-1/2 teaspoons smoked paprika

1 teaspoon salt

2 tablespoons olive oil

This tender pork loin is paired perfectly with the earthy flavor of mustard for a dish that is sure to please guests or you family. The addition of a little smoked paprika compliments the robust mustard and delicate pork tenderloin.

DIRECTIONS

1. In a small bowl, combine the mustard and paprika.
2. Set your griddle to medium heat.
3. Rub the tenderloins with the mustard mixture, making sure they are evenly coated.
4. Place the tenderloins on the griddle and cook until all sides are well browned, and the internal temperature is 135°F.
5. Remove the tenderloins from the griddle and rest 5 minutes before slicing and serving.

Nutritional Info: Calories: 484, Sodium: 755mg, Dietary Fiber: 4.2g, Fat: 24.7g, Carbs: 13.8g, Protein: 50.9g.

MOROCCAN SPICED PORK TENDERLOIN WITH CREAMY HARISSA SAUCE

SERVINGS: 6

Prep time: 40 minutes
Cook time: 20 minutes

INGREDIENTS

2 (1 lb.) pork tenderloins

1 teaspoon ground cinnamon

1 teaspoon ground cilantro

1 teaspoon ground cumin

1 teaspoon paprika

1 teaspoon sea salt

2 tablespoons olive oil

FOR CREAMY HARISSA SAUCE:

1 cup Greek yogurt (8 ounces)

1 tablespoon fresh lemon juice

1 tablespoon extra-virgin olive oil

1 teaspoon harissa sauce

1 clove garlic, minced

Kosher salt and cracked black pepper

Moroccan spice and creamy harissa make for one delicious way to serve up tender pork any night of the week. Enjoy this yummy dish with collard greens and potato salad for a taste twist on your next cookout.

DIRECTIONS

1. Combine harissa ingredients in a small mixing bowl and set aside.
2. Combine the cinnamon, coriander, cumin, paprika, salt and olive oil.
3. Rub the seasonings evenly over the pork tenderloins; cover and refrigerate for 30 minutes.
4. Preheat griddle to high heat and cook tenderloins until browned; about 8 to 10 minutes.
5. Turn and cook an additional 8 to 10 minutes. Transfer the tenderloins to a cutting board, tent with foil and rest for 10 minutes.
6. Slice and serve with creamy harissa sauce.

Nutritional Info: Calories: 376, Sodium: 458mg, Dietary Fiber: 0.4g, Fat: 17.9g, Carbs: 2.6g, Protein: 48.7g.

STICKY-SWEET PORK SHOULDER

SERVINGS: 6 - 8

Prep time: 8 hours
Cook time: 8 minutes

INGREDIENTS

1 (5 lbs.) Boston Butt pork shoulder

FOR THE MARINADE:

2 tablespoons garlic, minced

1 large piece ginger, peeled and chopped

1 cup hoisin sauce

3/4 cup fish sauce

2/3 cup honey

2/3 cup Shaoxing

1/2 cup chili oil

1/3 cup oyster sauce

1/3 cup sesame oil

FOR THE GLAZE:

3/4 cup dark brown sugar

1 tablespoon light molasses

Sweet and sticky sauce is the perfect complement to savory grilled pork. Serve this delicious dish with your favorite sides or as a delicious stuffing for steamed buns or grilled bread.

DIRECTIONS

1. Place pork shoulder, fat side down, on a cutting board with a short end facing you. Holding a long sharp knife about 1"–1-1/2" above cutting board, make a shallow cut along the entire length of a long side of shoulder.

2. Continue cutting deeper into meat, lifting and unfurling with your free hand, until it lies flat.

3. Purée marinade in a blender and reserve 1-1/2 cups for glaze, cover and refrigerate.

4. Pour remaining marinade in a large sealable plastic bag.

5. Add pork shoulder to bag and marinate in the refrigerator for 8 hours.

6. Preheat griddle to medium heat (with cover closed, thermometer should register 350°). Remove pork from marinade, letting excess drip off.

7. Add glaze ingredients to reserved marinade until sugar is dissolved.

8. Grill pork, for 8 minutes, basting and turning with tongs every minute or so, until thick coated with glaze, lightly charred in spots, and warmed through; an instant-read thermometer inserted into the thickest part should register 145°F.

9. Transfer to a cutting board and slice against the grain, 1/4" thick, to serve.

Nutritional Info: Calories: 1286, Sodium: 2875mg, Dietary Fiber: 1g, Fat: 84.8g, Carbs: 58.3g, Protein: 68.7g.

GRILLED PORK CHOPS WITH HERB APPLE COMPOTE

SERVINGS: 4

Prep time: 5 minutes
Cook time: 20 minutes

INGREDIENTS

4, bone-in pork chops

2 honeycrisp apples, peeled, cored and chopped

1/3 cup orange juice

1 teaspoon chopped fresh rosemary

1 teaspoon chopped fresh sage

Sea salt

Black pepper

Apples are one of my absolute favorite ingredients to pair with pork chops, and I hope you love this recipe too! Sweet meets juicy pork for a grilling flavor that is out of this world.

DIRECTIONS

1. Add the apples, herbs and orange juice to a saucepan and simmer over medium heat until the apples are tender and the juices are thickened to a thin syrup, about 10 to 12 minutes.
2. Season pork chops with salt and pepper.
3. Place on the griddle and cook until the pork chop releases from the griddle, about 4 minutes.
4. Flip and cook on the other side for 3 minutes.
5. Transfer to a cutting board and tent with foil.
6. Top with apple compote and serve!

Nutritional Info: Calories: 284, Sodium: 173mg, Dietary Fiber: 1g, Fat: 20g, Carbs: 7.2g, Protein: 18.2g.

YUCATAN-STYLE GRILLED PORK

SERVINGS: 4

Prep time: 15 minutes
Cook time: 8 minutes

Elevate simple grilled pork with Yucatan citrus combinations to make something different on your outdoor griddle Serve this with a side of grilled plantains, veggies, and sparkling water.

INGREDIENTS

2 pork tenderloins, trimmed
1 teaspoon annatto powder
Olive oil

FOR THE MARINADE:

2 oranges, juiced
2 lemons, juiced, or more to taste
2 limes, juiced, or more to taste
6 cloves garlic, minced
1 teaspoon ground cumin
1/2 teaspoon cayenne pepper
1/2 teaspoon dried oregano
1/2 teaspoon black pepper

DIRECTIONS

1. Combine marinade ingredients in a mixing bowl and whisk until well-blended.
2. Cut the tenderloins in half crosswise; cut each piece in half lengthwise.
3. Place pieces in marinade and thoroughly coat with the mixture.
4. Cover with plastic wrap and refrigerate 4 to 6 hours.
5. Transfer pieces of pork from marinade to a paper-towel-lined bowl to absorb most of the moisture.
6. Discard paper towels. Drizzle olive oil and a bit more annatto powder on the pork.
7. Preheat griddle for medium-high heat and lightly oil.
8. Place pieces evenly spaced on griddle; cook 4 to 5 minutes.
9. Turn and cook on the other side another 4 or 5 minutes.
10. Transfer onto a serving platter and allow meat to rest about 5 minutes before serving.

Nutritional Info: Calories: 439, Sodium: 1382mg, Dietary Fiber: 1.5g, Fat: 33.1g, Carbs: 11.4g, Protein: 23.9g.

PINEAPPLE BACON PORK CHOPS

SERVINGS: 6

Prep time: 30 minutes
Cook time: 1 hour

INGREDIENTS

1 large whole pineapple
6 pork chops
12 slices thick-cut bacon
Toothpicks, soaked in water

FOR THE GLAZE:
1/4 cup honey
1/8 teaspoon cayenne pepper

Sweet and juicy pineapple compliments savory pork for one incredible dish! You'll love the sweet and spicy kick in this recipe - serve it with your favorite grilled side dishes and vegetables and a cold glass of beer or iced tea.

DIRECTIONS

1. Turn both burners to medium-high heat; after about 15 minutes, turn off one of the middle burners and turn the remaining burners down to medium.
2. Slice off the top and bottom of the pineapple, and peel the pineapple, cutting the skin off in strips.
3. Cut pineapple flesh into six quarters.
4. Wrap each pineapple section with a bacon slice; secure each end with a toothpick.
5. Brush quarters with honey and sprinkle with cayenne pepper.
6. Put the quarters on the griddle, flipping when bacon is cooked so that both sides are evenly grilled.
7. While pineapple quarters are cooking, coat pork chops with honey and cayenne pepper. Set on griddle.
8. Tent with foil and cook for 20 minutes. Flip, and continue cooking an additional 10 to 20 minutes or until chops are fully cooked.
9. Serve each chop with a pineapple quarter on the side.

Nutritional Info: Calories: 380, Sodium: 852mg, Dietary Fiber: 0.5g, Fat: 23.5g, Carbs: 18.2g, Protein: 25.8g.

GLAZED COUNTRY RIBS

SERVINGS: 6

Prep time: 10 minutes
Cook time: 4 hours

INGREDIENTS

3 pounds country-style pork ribs

1 cup low-sugar ketchup

1/2 cup water

1/4 cup onion, finely chopped

1/4 cup cider vinegar or wine vinegar

1/4 cup light molasses

2 tablespoons Worcestershire sauce

2 teaspoons chili powder

2 cloves garlic, minced

Country ribs are full of delicious flavor and make for one great main dish on weeknights or weekends with friends. Serve these ribs with your favorite sides and cold, crisp beer on summer holidays for traditional grilling fun.

DIRECTIONS

1. Combine ketchup, water, onion, vinegar, molasses, Worcestershire sauce, chili powder, and garlic in a saucepan and bring to boil; reduce heat. Simmer, uncovered, for 10 to 15 minutes or until desired thickness is reached, stirring often.
2. Trim fat from ribs.
3. Preheat griddle to medium-high.
4. Place ribs, bone-side down, on griddle and cook for 1-1/2 to 2 hours or until tender, brushing occasionally with sauce during the last 10 minutes of cooking.
5. Serve with remaining sauce and enjoy!

Nutritional Info: Calories: 404, Sodium: 733mg, Dietary Fiber: 0.4g, Fat: 8.1g, Carbs: 15.2g, Protein: 60.4g.

GARLIC SOY PORK CHOPS

SERVINGS: 4 - 6

Prep time: 8 hours
Cook time: 1 hour

Sweet and spicy ribs are a great way to grill out with the whole family on the weekends. Serve these sticky ribs with mashed potatoes and grilled vegetables for some decadent weekend backyard fun.

INGREDIENTS

- 4 to 6 pork chops
- 4 cloves garlic, finely chopped
- 1/2 cup olive oil
- 1/2 cup soy sauce
- 1/2 teaspoon garlic powder
- 1/2 teaspoon salt
- 1/2 black pepper
- 1/4 cup butter

DIRECTIONS

1. In a large zipper lock bag, combine the garlic, olive oil, soy sauce, and garlic powder. Add the pork chops and make sure the marinade coats the chops. Set aside for 30 minutes.

2. Heat your griddle to medium-high heat. Add 2 tablespoons of olive oil and 2 tablespoons of butter to the griddle.

3. Add the chops to the griddle one at a time, making sure they are not crowded. Add another 2 tablespoons of butter to the griddle and cook the chops for 4 minutes. Cook an additional 4 minutes.

4. Remove the chops from the griddle and spread the remaining butter over them. Serve after resting for 5 minutes.

Nutritional Info: Calories: 398, Sodium: 1484mg, Dietary Fiber: 0.2g, Fat: 37.7g, Carbs: 2.5g, Protein: 13.6g.

HONEY SOY PORK CHOPS

SERVINGS: 6

Prep time: 1 hour
Cook time: 25 minutes

INGREDIENTS

6 (4 ounce) boneless pork chops

1/4 cup organic honey

1 to 2 tablespoons low sodium soy sauce

2 tablespoons olive oil

1 tablespoon rice mirin

Sweet and tangy grilled pork is absolutely delicious when grilled to perfection on your outdoor griddle. Simply serve this dish with rice and grilled vegetables for one delicious meal.

DIRECTIONS

1. Combine honey, soy sauce, oil, and white vinegar and whisk until well-combined. Add sauce and pork chops to a large sealable plastic bag and marinate for 1 hour.

2. Preheat the griddle to medium-high heat and cook for 4 to 5 minutes, or until the pork chop easily releases from the griddle.

3. Flip and continue to cook for 5 additional minutes, or until internal temperature reaches 145°F.

4. Serve and enjoy!

Nutritional Info: Calories: 251, Sodium: 187mg, Dietary Fiber: 0.1g, Fat: 8.7g, Carbs: 13.1g, Protein: 29.9g.

HABANERO-MARINATED PORK CHOPS

SERVINGS: 4

Prep time: 30 minutes
Cook time: 13 minutes

INGREDIENTS

4-1/2-inch-thick bone-in pork chops

3 tablespoons olive oil, plus more for grill

Kosher salt and freshly ground black pepper

FOR THE MARINADE:

1 habanero chili, seeded, chopped fine

2 garlic cloves, minced

1/2 cup fresh orange juice

2 tablespoons brown sugar

1 tablespoon apple cider vinegar

Kick things up a notch on your outdoor griddle with this spicy recipe. These yummy pork chops pair perfectly with yellow rice, black beans, and your favorite salad.

DIRECTIONS

1. Combine marinade ingredients in a large sealable plastic bag.
2. Pierce pork chops all over with a fork and add to bag, seal, and turn to coat.
3. Marinate at room temperature, turning occasionally, for 30 minutes.
4. Prepare griddle for medium-high heat.
5. Brush the griddle with oil.
6. Remove pork chops from marinade and pat dry.
7. Sear for 8 minutes, turning occasionally, until charred and cooked through.
8. Transfer to a plate and let rest 5 minutes.
9. Serve with your favorite sides.

Nutritional Info: Calories: 490, Sodium: 171mg, Dietary Fiber: 1.1g, Fat: 39.2g, Carbs: 10.9g, Protein: 23.3g.

CUBAN PORK CHOPS

SERVINGS: 4

Prep time: 30 minutes
Cook time: 1 hour 30 minutes

INGREDIENTS

4 pork chops

4 cloves garlic, smashed

2 tablespoons olive oil

1/3 cup lime juice

1/4 cup water

1 teaspoon ground cumin

Salt and black pepper

These authentic Cuban pork chops are easy to make and packed with exotic flavors. Thanks to your outdoor griddle they are sure to cook to perfection.

DIRECTIONS

1. Set your griddle to medium. Salt the pork chops on both side and cook the chops until lightly browned.
2. Combine the water, garlic, and lime juice in a bowl and whisk until even.
3. Continue cooking the pork chops while basting them with the lime juice mixture.
4. When the pork chops have finished cooking, remove from the griddle and top with additional sauce and black pepper before serving.

Nutritional Info: Calories: 323, Sodium: 58mg, Dietary Fiber: 0.1g, Fat: 27g, Carbs: 1.5g, Protein: 18.3g.

SPICY CAJUN PORK CHOPS

SERVINGS: 4

Prep time: 10 minutes
Cook time: 15 minutes

INGREDIENTS

4 pork chops

1 tablespoon paprika

1/2 teaspoon ground cumin

1/2 teaspoon dried sage

1/2 teaspoon salt

1/2 teaspoon black pepper

1/2 teaspoon garlic powder

1/4 teaspoon cayenne pepper

1 tablespoon butter

1 tablespoon vegetable oil

Packed with flavor and a nice amount of heat, these Cajun pork chops are perfect for outdoor cooking any time of year. For best results, serve with a nice, rich coleslaw.

DIRECTIONS

1. In a medium bowl, combine the paprika, cumin, sage, salt, pepper, garlic, and cayenne pepper.
2. Heat your griddle to medium-high heat and add the butter and oil.
3. Rub the pork chops with a generous amount of the seasoning rub.
4. Place the chops on the griddle and cook for 4 to 5 minutes. Turn the pork chops and continue cooking an additional 4 minutes.
5. Remove the pork chops from the griddle and allow to rest 5 minutes before serving.

Nutritional Info: Calories: 320, Sodium: 368mg, Dietary Fiber: 0.8g, Fat: 26.5g, Carbs: 1.6g, Protein: 18.4g.

CHAPTER 9

MAIN DISHES: SEAFOOD

SALMON FILLETS WITH BASIL BUTTER & BROCCOLINI

SERVINGS: 2

Prep time: 10 minutes
Cook time: 12 minutes

INGREDIENTS

2 (6 ounce) salmon fillets, skin removed

2 tablespoons butter, unsalted

2 basil leaves, minced

1 garlic clove, minced

6 ounces broccolini

2 teaspoons olive oil

Sea salt, to taste

Basil infused broccoli is the perfect way to elevate seared salmon. Healthy and delicious, this recipe is also easy to make on those busy weeknights when you still want a decadent tasting dinner.

DIRECTIONS

1. Blend butter, basil, and garlic together until well-incorporated. Form into a ball and place in refrigerator until ready to serve.
2. Preheat griddle to medium-high heat.
3. Season both sides of the salmon fillets with salt and set aside.
4. Add broccolini, a pinch of salt, and olive oil to a bowl, toss to coat, and set aside.
5. Brush griddle with olive oil, and cook salmon, skin side down, for 12 minutes. Turn the salmon and cook for an additional 4 minutes. Remove from the griddle and allow to rest while the broccolini cooks.
6. Add the broccolini to the griddle, turning occasionally, until slightly charred, about 6 minutes.
7. Top each salmon fillet with a slice of basil butter and serve with a side of broccolini.

Nutritional Info: Calories: 398, Sodium: 303mg, Dietary Fiber: 2.2g, Fat: 26.7g, Carbs: 6.2g, Protein: 35.6g.

SPICED SNAPPER WITH MANGO AND RED ONION SALAD

SERVINGS: 4

Prep time: 10 minutes
Cook time: 20 minutes

INGREDIENTS

2 red snappers, cleaned

Sea salt

1/3 cup tandoori spice

Olive oil, plus more for grill

Extra-virgin olive oil, for drizzling

Lime wedges, for serving

FOR THE SALSA:

1 ripe but firm mango, peeled and chopped

1 small red onion, thinly sliced

1 bunch cilantro, coarsely chopped

3 tablespoons fresh lime juice

Spiced snapper meets cool, crisp mango salad for one delicious way to grill up lunch. Serve this gorgeous seafood feast with sparkling water with lemon and warm baguettes for a delicious lunch in the sun.

DIRECTIONS

1. Toss mango, onion, cilantro, lime juice, and a big pinch of salt in a medium mixing bowl; drizzle with a bit of olive oil and toss again to coat.
2. Place snapper on a cutting board and pat dry with paper towels. Cut slashes crosswise on a diagonal along the body every 2" on both sides, with a sharp knife, cutting all the way down to the bones.
3. Season fish generously inside and out with salt. Coat fish with tandoori spice.
4. Preheat griddle medium-high heat and brush with oil.
5. Grill fish for 10 minutes, undisturbed, until skin is puffed and charred.
6. Flip and grill fish until the other side is lightly charred and skin is puffed, about 8 to 12 minutes.
7. Transfer to a platter.
8. Top with mango salad and serve with lime wedges.

Nutritional Info: Calories: 211, Sodium: 170mg, Dietary Fiber: 2.5g, Fat: 5.4g, Carbs: 18.9g, Protein: 23.6g.

HONEY-LIME TILAPIA AND CORN FOIL PACK

SERVINGS: 4

Prep time: 10 minutes
Cook time: 10 minutes

INGREDIENTS

4 fillets tilapia

2 tablespoons honey

4 limes, thinly sliced

2 ears corn, shucked

2 tablespoons fresh cilantro leaves

1/4 cup olive oil

Kosher salt

Freshly ground black pepper

The sweet taste of honey and citrus lime come together to infuse flaky tilapia with a flavor sensation out of this world. Serve these yummy foil packs with garden salads and your favorite sparkling beverage.

DIRECTIONS

1. Preheat griddle to high.
2. Cut 4 squares of foil about 12" long.
3. Top each piece of foil with a piece of tilapia.
4. Brush tilapia with honey and top with lime, corn and cilantro.
5. Drizzle with olive oil and season with sea salt and pepper.
6. Cook until tilapia is cooked through and corn tender, about 15 minutes.

Nutritional Info: Calories: 319, Sodium: 92mg, Dietary Fiber: 4g, Fat: 14.7g, Carbs: 30.3g, Protein: 24g.

HALIBUT FILLETS WITH SPINACH AND OLIVES

SERVINGS: 4

Prep time: 10 minutes
Cook time: 10 minutes

INGREDIENTS

4 (6 ounce) halibut fillets
1/3 cup olive oil
4 cups baby spinach
1/4 cup lemon juice
2 ounces pitted black olives, halved
2 tablespoons flat leaf parsley, chopped
2 teaspoons fresh dill, chopped
Lemon wedges, to serve

Fresh, flaky fish is perfect served with salty olives and fresh spinach. This recipe makes for one quick and easy dinner any day of the week!

DIRECTIONS

1. Preheat griddle to medium heat.
2. Toss spinach with lemon juice in a mixing bowl and set aside.
3. Brush fish with olive oil and cook for 3-4 minutes per side, or until cooked through.
4. Remove from heat, cover with foil and let rest for 5 minutes.
5. Add remaining oil and cook spinach for 2 minutes, or until just wilted. Remove from heat.
6. Toss with olives and herbs, then transfer to serving plates with fish, and serve with lemon wedges.

Nutritional Info: Calories: 773, Sodium: 1112mg, Dietary Fiber: 1.4g, Fat: 36.6g, Carbs: 2.9g, Protein: 109.3g.

SPICED CRAB LEGS

SERVINGS: 4

Prep time: 5 minutes
Cook time: 5 minutes

INGREDIENTS

4 lbs king crab legs, cooked

2 tablespoons chili oil

Crab legs with a twist! If you love spice, you'll love this recipe - but on the chance you just love crab legs you can also substitute chili for olive oil and try it hot and mild!

DIRECTIONS

1. Preheat griddle to high.
2. Brush both sides of crab legs with chili oil and place on grill. Tent with foil.
3. Cook 4 to 5 minutes, turning once.
4. Transfer to plates and serve with drawn butter.

Nutritional Info: Calories: 518, Sodium: 4857mg, Dietary Fiber: 0g, Fat: 13.9g, Carbs: 0g, Protein: 87.1g.

GREMOLATA SWORDFISH SKEWERS

SERVINGS: 4

Prep time: 20 minutes
Cook time: 10 minutes

INGREDIENTS

1-1/2 lb. skinless swordfish fillet

2 teaspoons lemon zest

3 tablespoons lemon juice

1/2 cup finely chopped parsley

2 teaspoons garlic, minced

3/4 teaspoon sea salt

1/4 teaspoon black pepper

2 tablespoons extra-virgin olive oil, plus extra for serving

1/2 teaspoon red pepper flakes

3 lemons, cut into slices

Delicate, flaky swordfish makes for one delicious grilled skewer! Serve your yummy swordfish with lemon chili pasta, salad, and Chardonnay or sparkling water with lemon.

DIRECTIONS

1. Preheat griddle to medium-high.
2. Combine lemon zest, parsley, garlic, 1/4 teaspoon of the salt, and pepper in a small bowl with a fork to make gremolata and set aside.
3. Mix swordfish pieces with reserved lemon juice, olive oil, red pepper flakes, and remaining salt.
4. Thread swordfish and lemon slices, alternating each, onto the metal skewers.
5. Grill skewers 8 to 10 minutes, flipping halfway through, or until fish is cooked through.
6. Place skewers on a serving platter and sprinkle with gremolata.
7. Drizzle with olive oil and serve.

Nutritional Info: Calories: 333, Sodium: 554mg, Dietary Fiber: 0.5g, Fat: 16g, Carbs: 1.6g, Protein: 43.7g.

LOBSTER TAILS WITH LIME BASIL BUTTER

SERVINGS: 4

Prep time: 5 minutes
Cook time: 6 minutes

INGREDIENTS

4 lobster tails (cut in half lengthwise)
3 tablespoons olive oil
Lime wedges (to serve)
Sea salt, to taste

FOR THE LIME BASIL BUTTER:
1 stick unsalted butter, softened
1/2 bunch basil, roughly chopped
1 lime, zested and juiced
2 cloves garlic, minced
1/4 teaspoon red pepper flakes

For one amazing dinner, fire up your outdoor griddle and you can grill up lobster tails in less than 10 minutes. Serve them with grilled vegetables, crab legs, and shrimp for a seafood feast.

DIRECTIONS

1. Add the butter ingredients to a mixing bowl and combine; set aside until ready to use.
2. Preheat griddle to medium-high heat.
3. Drizzle the lobster tail halves with olive oil and season with salt and pepper.
4. Place the lobster tails, flesh-side down, on the griddle.
5. Allow to cook until opaque, about 3 minutes, flip and cook another 3 minutes.
6. Add a dollop of the lime basil butter during the last minute of cooking.
7. Serve immediately.

Nutritional Info: Calories: 430, Sodium: 926mg, Dietary Fiber: 0.5g, Fat: 34.7g, Carbs: 2.4g, Protein: 28g.

LUMP CRAB CAKES

SERVINGS: 4

Prep time: 10 minutes
Cook time: 15 minutes

INGREDIENTS

1 lb lump crab meat

1/2 cup panko breadcrumbs

1/3 cup mayonnaise

1 egg, beaten

2 tablespoons Dijon mustard

2 teaspoons Worcestershire sauce

1/2 teaspoon paprika

1/2 teaspoon salt

1/4 teaspoon black pepper

3 tablespoons vegetable oil

Cooking crab cakes on your outdoor griddle is a no brainer because of the perfectly controlled and even heat the flat top surface offers. These crab cakes are bursting with flavors the whole family will love.

DIRECTIONS

1. Preheat griddle to medium heat.
2. In a large bowl, combine the crab, breadcrumbs, mayo, egg, mustard Worcestershire sauce, paprika, salt and pepper. Mix well to combine.
3. Form the crab mixture into 4 large balls and flatten them slightly.
4. Add the oil to the griddle and cook the crab cakes for approximately 5 minutes per side or until browned and crispy. Serve immediately.

Nutritional Info: Calories: 282, Sodium: 1205mg, Dietary Fiber: 0.6g, Fat: 27.4g, Carbs: 9.5g, Protein: 18.8g.

SPICY GRILLED JUMBO SHRIMP

SERVINGS: 6

Prep time: 15 minutes
Cook time: 8 minutes

INGREDIENTS

1-1/2 pounds uncooked jumbo shrimp, peeled and deveined

FOR THE MARINADE:

2 tablespoons fresh parsley
1 bay leaf, dried
1 teaspoon chili powder
1 teaspoon garlic powder
1/4 teaspoon cayenne pepper
1/4 cup olive oil
1/4 teaspoon salt
1/8 teaspoon pepper

Spicy grilled shrimp is just out of this world! Top your favorite salads, yellow rice and vegetables, or even serve it on its own for grilling fun.

DIRECTIONS

1. Add marinade ingredients to a food processor and process until smooth.
2. Transfer marinade to a large mixing bowl.
3. Fold in shrimp and toss to coat; refrigerate, covered, 30 minutes.
4. Thread shrimp onto metal skewers.
5. Preheat griddle to medium heat.
6. Cook 5-6 minutes, flipping once, until shrimp turn opaque pink.
7. Serve immediately.

Nutritional Info: Calories: 131, Sodium: 980mg, Dietary Fiber: 0.4g, Fat: 8.5g, Carbs: 1g, Protein: 13.7g.

COCONUT PINEAPPLE SHRIMP SKEWERS

SERVINGS: 4

Prep time: 1 hour 20 minutes
Cook time: 5 minutes

INGREDIENTS

1-1/2 pounds uncooked jumbo shrimp, peeled and deveined

1/2 cup light coconut milk

1 tablespoon cilantro, chopped

4 teaspoons Tabasco Original Red Sauce

2 teaspoons soy sauce

1/4 cup freshly squeezed orange juice

1/4 cup freshly squeezed lime juice (from about 2 large limes)

3/4 pound pineapple, cut into 1 inch chunks

Olive oil, for grilling

Creamy coconut and fresh pineapple come together to create a taste of Thailand. Serve this decadent shrimp on top a bed of mango sticky rice for one delicious meal.

DIRECTIONS

1. Combine the coconut milk, cilantro, Tabasco sauce, soy sauce, orange juice, lime juice. Add the shrimp and toss to coat.
2. Cover and place in the refrigerator to marinate for 1 hour.
3. Thread shrimp and pineapple onto metal skewers, alternating each.
4. Preheat griddle to medium heat.
5. Cook 5-6 minutes, flipping once, until shrimp turn opaque pink.
6. Serve immediately.

Nutritional Info: Calories: 150, Sodium: 190mg, Dietary Fiber: 1.9g, Fat: 10.8g, Carbs: 14.9g, Protein: 1.5g.

MEXICAN SHRIMP TACOS

SERVINGS: 4

Prep Time: 10 minutes
Cook Time: 10 minutes

INGREDIENTS

2 lbs. medium shrimp, peeled and deveined

8 flour tortillas, warmed

1 bag cabbage slaw

1 cup salsa

1 cup Mexican crema

FOR MARINADE:

2 tablespoons olive oil

1 tablespoon chili powder

1 tablespoon cumin

1 tablespoon garlic powder

1 tablespoon fresh lime juice

1/4 teaspoon sea salt

1/8 teaspoon fresh ground pepper

Shrimp tacos are a great way to whip up a healthy dinner in no time for the whole family. These tacos are spiced to perfection and will definitely become a family favorite in no time!

DIRECTIONS

1. Preheat a griddle to medium-high.
2. Combine oil marinade in a large sealable plastic bag. Add shrimp and toss coat; let marinate in the refrigerator for 30 minutes.
3. Cook shrimp for 3 minutes, on each side, until cooked through.
4. Transfer to a plate.
5. Lay two tortillas on each plate. Evenly divide the shrimp, cabbage slaw, salsa in the middle of each tortilla.
6. Drizzle with Mexican crema and serve.

Nutritional Info: Calories: 400, Sodium: 92mg, Dietary Fiber: 4g, Fat: 14.7g, Carbs: 30.3g, Protein: 24g.

BACON WRAPPED SCALLOPS

SERVINGS: 4

Prep time: 15 minutes
Cook time: 4 minutes

INGREDIENTS

12 large sea scallops, side muscle removed

8 slices of bacon

1 tablespoon vegetable oil

12 toothpicks

The delicate, sweet flavor of fresh sea scallops pairs perfectly with the rich salty flavor of bacon. And best of all, you can prepare this entire meal on your outdoor griddle.

DIRECTIONS

1. Heat your griddle to medium heat and cook the bacon until fat has rendered but bacon is still flexible. Remove bacon from the griddle and place on paper towels.
2. Raise griddle heat to medium-high.
3. Wrap each scallop with a half slice of bacon and skewer with a toothpick to keep the bacon in place.
4. Place the scallops on the griddle and cook for 90 seconds per side. They should be lightly browned on both sides.
5. Remove from the griddle and serve immediately.

Nutritional Info: Calories: 315, Sodium: 1023mg, Dietary Fiber: 0g, Fat: 20g, Carbs: 2.7g, Protein: 29.2g.

SCALLOPS WITH LEMONY SALSA VERDE

SERVINGS: 2

Prep time: 10 minutes
Cook time: 5 minutes

Brighten up your grilled scallops with a citrus-infused Salsa Verde. Lemony Salsa Verde is the perfect complement to hearty scallops and delicious served alongside risotto or a gorgeous salad.

INGREDIENTS

1 tablespoon olive oil, plus more for grilling

12 large sea scallops, side muscle removed

Sea salt, for seasoning

FOR THE LEMONY SALSA VERDE:

1/2 lemon, with peel, seeded and chopped

5 tomatillos, peeled and pulsed in a blender

1 small shallot, finely chopped

1 garlic clove, finely chopped

1/4 cup olive oil

3/4 cup finely chopped fresh parsley

1/2 cup finely chopped fresh cilantro

1/4 cup chopped fresh chives

1/4 teaspoon sea salt

1/4 teaspoon black pepper

DIRECTIONS

1. Toss Lemony Salsa ingredients in a small mixing bowl and set aside.
2. Preheat griddle for medium-high and brush with olive oil.
3. Toss scallops with 1 tablespoon olive oil on a baking sheet and season with salt.
4. Add scallops to griddle, turning once after 45 seconds to 1 minute. Cook an additional 1 minute before removing from the griddle.
5. Serve scallops topped with Lemony Salsa Verde.

Nutritional Info: Calories: 267, Sodium: 541mg, Dietary Fiber: 3.1g, Fat: 9.6g, Carbs: 13.9g, Protein: 32.4g.

GRILLED OYSTERS WITH SPICED TEQUILA BUTTER

SERVINGS: 6

Prep time: 5 minutes
Cook time: 25 minutes

INGREDIENTS

3 dozen medium oysters, scrubbed and shucked

Flakey sea salt, for serving

FOR THE BUTTER:

1/4 teaspoon crushed red pepper

7 tablespoons unsalted butter

1/4 teaspoon chili oil

1 teaspoon dried oregano

2 tablespoons freshly squeezed lemon juice

2 tablespoons Tequila Blanco, like Espolon

Tequila infused butter is just the way to elevate oysters fresh off the grill. A delicious appetizer, these oysters are also yummy served with a glass of Sauvignon Blanc or crisp lager and French fries.

DIRECTIONS

1. Combine butter ingredients in a small mixing bowl until well-incorporated and set aside.
2. Preheat griddle to high.
3. Grill the oysters about 1 to 2 minutes.
4. Sprinkle the oysters with salt flakes.
5. Warm the butter in a microwave for 30 seconds, and spoon the warm Tequila butter over the oysters and serve.

Nutritional Info: Calories: 184, Sodium: 300mg, Dietary Fiber: 0.2g, Fat: 15g, Carbs: 3.8g, Protein: 0.2g.

POP-OPEN CLAMS WITH HORSERADISH-TABASCO SAUCE

SERVINGS: 4

Prep time: 5 minutes
Cook time: 10 minutes

These spicy clams are a great way to serve up some decadent seafood right at home. Best served with crusty grilled bread, you'll love this delicious recipe as a starter or side to the perfect dinner.

INGREDIENTS

2 dozen littleneck clams, scrubbed
4 tablespoons unsalted butter, softened
2 tablespoons horseradish, drained
1 tablespoon hot sauce, like Tabasco
1/4 teaspoon lemon zest, finely grated
1 tablespoon fresh lemon juice
1/4 teaspoon smoked paprika
Sea salt

DIRECTIONS

1. Preheat the griddle to high.
2. Blend the butter with the horseradish, hot sauce, lemon zest, lemon juice, paprika, and pinch of salt.
3. Arrange the clams over high heat and grill until they pop open, about 25 seconds.
4. Carefully turn the clams over using tongs, so the meat side is down.
5. Grill for about 20 seconds longer, until the clam juices start to simmer.
6. Transfer the clams to a serving bowl.
7. Top each with about 1/2 teaspoon of the sauce and serve.

Nutritional Info: Calories: 191, Sodium: 382mg, Dietary Fiber: 0.3g, Fat: 12.7g, Carbs: 4g, Protein: 14.8g.

SPICY GRILLED SQUID

SERVINGS: 4

Prep time: 5 minutes
Cook time: 5 minutes

INGREDIENTS

1-1/2 lbs. Squid, prepared
Olive oil

FOR THE MARINADE:

2 cloves garlic cloves, minced
1/2 teaspoon ginger, minced
3 tablespoons gochujang
3 tablespoons corn syrup
1 teaspoon yellow mustard
1 teaspoon soy sauce
2 teaspoons sesame oil
1 teaspoon sesame seeds
2 green onions, chopped

Spice things up with this yummy recipe and serve up some squid at your next dinner party. The perfect appetizer, this is best served on its own or as a decadent appetizer on a bed of leafy greens.

DIRECTIONS

1. Preheat griddle to medium high heat and brush with olive oil.
2. Add the squid and tentacles to the griddle and cook for 1 minute until the bottom looks firm and opaque.
3. Turn them over and cook for another minute; straighten out the body with tongs if it curls.
4. Baste with sauce on top of the squid and cook 2 additional minutes.
5. Flip and baste the other side, cook 1 minute until the sauce evaporates and the squid turns red and shiny.

Nutritional Info: Calories: 292, Sodium: 466mg, Dietary Fiber: 2.7g, Fat: 8.6g, Carbs: 25.1g, Protein: 27.8g.

KITCHEN UNIT CONVERSION

1 teaspoon	= 1/3 tbsp	= 4.9 ml
1 dessertspoon	= 2 tsp	= 9.9 ml
1 tablespoon	= 1.5 dstsp / 3 tsp	= 14.8 ml
1 fuid ounce	= 2 tbsp / 6 tsp	= 29.6 ml
1 cup	= 16 tbsp / 48 tsp	= 236.6 ml
1 quart	= 4 cup	= 946 ml
1 gal	= 4 quart / 16 cup	= 3.79 l
1 ounce	= 2 tbsp	= 28.4 g
1 pounds	= 16 oz	= 453.6 g

www.ingramcontent.com/pod-product-compliance
Lightning Source LLC
Chambersburg PA
CBHW051804100526
44592CB00016B/2553